D0576367

RIGHT

on the

MONEY

**Wealth-building wisdom from the world's
most popular financial adviser**

LOUIS RUKEYSER

© *1998 Financial Service Associates, L.P., 1750 Old Meadow Rd., Suite 300, McLean, VA 22102.*

TABLE OF CONTENTS

INTRODUCTION

Oddly, though the stock market has been the single best place for the average American to make money over the decades, it is pessimistic commentary that usually arrests people's attention. As I note in these pages, the least-accurate predictors throughout the nearly three decades I've been doing *Wall $treet Week With Louis Rukeyser* have been—by an embarrassingly wide margin—the perennial gloomsters. They prey, consciously or otherwise, on people's natural anxieties about money. Fear beats greed by a landslide when the going gets tough. Even though the stock market historically rises two days out of three, and proceeds inexorably upward over the generations, its bad down days tend not only to be more dramatic but to be treated with considerably greater prominence by many in the news media, either because of their famous ignorance about fundamental economics or simply because they are aware that horror and panic will always sell better than sensible reassurance.

Hence it may come as a surprise to some readers to see how extraordinarily profitable the basically optimistic commentaries collected in this book have turned out to be. Optimism is rarely fashionable in money matters (it is conventionally derided as Pollyannaish wishful thinking), yet it has been, in retrospect, the only genuine realism for serious investors. Optimism does not translate into naïveté; the optimist knows at least as well as the pessimist that occasional violent selloffs are a natural accompaniment to the market's long-term progress, and is prepared in advance to ride them out—buying where possible, holding where not. It's not that the rational optimist is never frightened or unhappy when the market dives as it did again in late 1998, it is that he or she knows that such interludes are not just inevitable but ultimately healthy: washing out temporary excesses and preparing the market for its next relentless surge upward.

The words in this book were not written for the ages, but for readers of my two monthly newsletters, *Louis Rukeyser's Wall Street* and *Louis Rukeyser's Mutual Funds*. The former was launched in January 1992 and the latter two years later, and they have already survived some extraordinary market cycles. My advice has long been that the traditional debate about which form of analysis is dominant in investing, technical (what the charts and graphs are saying) or fundamental (how the company and the economy are actually doing), overlooks the form of analysis that more truly dominates the market in the short term: psychoanalysis. The market's mood can turn in a millisecond from headlong euphoria to mindless despair. This is enough to send some people racing permanently for the exits, but it should really upset only those who are investing with borrowed money (margin), treating the market like a casino (options) or paying attention to the ever-overexposed hysterics (idiots). For the rest of us, it adds a little excitement to our lives for a while, but does not deter us from the task of steadily constructing our fortunes. I hope you're in that group, and if not, will join it pronto. The wealth you build will be your own.

If, like me, you're old-fashioned enough to read a book's Table of Contents, you'll see that this one is divided into three sections. The first two are selections made by our editors from the two-page opening commentaries that are at the front of each of the newsletters each month. In every case, you'll find the date that the commentary originally appeared. (We leave the con jobs and the backdating of predictions to others, who love to claim that they have called every single short-term market movement since the death of Alexander Hamilton. Feel free to enjoy their prose, as I do; in my present professional incarnation, I don't get to read a lot of fiction.) The first section empha-sizes enduring investment strategies. The second covers the economy, government and politics—the inescapable background for the market's eventual behavior. And the final section contains relevant excerpts from The Rukeyser Interview, an in-depth talk with one of the mar-ket's top performers, which is also a monthly feature of both newsletters.

I hope you'll enjoy the book and find it rewarding. Sound investing advice is often timeless, and that's what we've aimed to bring you here. But as I write herein, an authentic secret of the stock market is that "every time is different." Conditions change, and so does the relative attractiveness of different securities and investments, so a sensible investor blends underlying optimism with continual vigilance, monitoring and reassessment. Thus your portfolio will change through the years but not your basic belief that—despite all passing indications to the contrary—we will ultimately not just muddle through but go on to much-greater prosperity. I'll be riding that happier train, and I hope you will, too.

Read 'em and reap!

With the bullish best wishes of

Louis Rukeyser

LOUIS RUKEYSER

on

INVESTING

PART ONE

Louis Rukeyser
on
Investing

From "Myth America: Correcting the Bull from the Bears"
—May 1996

Six myths to ignore as you continue to make money in the great bull market:

(1) The little guy has gone crazy, buying stocks like never before and succumbing to a euphoria that can only end in disaster.

This argument will, I'm sure, sound familiar to you, as it is repeated so often by the financial magazines, newspapers and media commentators whose most distinguishing characteristic is how badly they have missed the record surge up to now. Since nothing seems to have gone the way they confidently predicted (i.e., way, way down), they soothe their egos by concluding that everything they have so totally misunderstood must, by definition, have been irrational.

You betcha. The reality, as usual, is quite different. Take, for example, the scary notion that a hysterical buying frenzy has led us poor, demented individual investors to put an unprecedented share of our savings into stocks. A terrible thought, isn't it? And it has every virtue except accuracy. Fact is, we're nowhere near record levels. Ownership of stocks, including stock mutual funds, as a percentage of total household financial assets is up significantly since 1982 (and thank goodness for that!), but it's still below 25%—nowhere near where it was for most of the 1950s and 1960s, when it peaked above 35%. Americans understandably fled from stocks during the stagflation 1970s, and they have only very slowly and cautiously been rebuilding sensible positions in that area. Runaway euphoria it certainly is not.

(2) Things may be OK now, but look out below when the baby boomers start to retire.

This myth is of newer vintage, but it has begun to show up in a number of publications conspicuous for having underrated the market's power in the past. The idea is that boomers have been pouring money into mutual funds, and this is why the market—otherwise unaccountably!—keeps going up. However, when the boomers start to retire and take out money in about 15 years, we'll all be clobbered in the rush for the exits. Again, it sounds frightening when you say it fast, but this one too collapses of its own weight when you examine those uncomfortable things known as facts. First, even if you accept the questionable premise, not all the baby boomers will be retiring on the same day, or in the same year; you'll have another full generation to assess the impact of their actions. Second, given the inability of these would-be sages to tell us with any precision where we're going to be next autumn, I am rudely skeptical of their ability to forecast exactly what's going to happen decades from now; there remains the excellent possibility that something else favorable to equities, economically and/or politically, may occur to counterbalance the expected sales by boomers. Third, and perhaps most embarrassing to those making this glib argument, they have greatly exaggerated the actual role of mutual funds in fueling this market advance.

While mutual-fund cash flow into equities has indeed been substantial ($120 billion in 1995 and $67.4 billion in the first quarter of 1996), it has been a less-important market factor than investments by corporations themselves. Announced mergers and acquisitions by U.S. firms alone totaled $400 billion last year and $105.7 billion in the first three months of 1996. This has been a dramatic prop under stock prices, and in fact has resulted in a shrinking supply of stocks—despite all the new issues that garner so much publicity. In the 14 months beginning in January 1995, the Securities Data Company reports, the supply of stocks was lowered by fully $235 billion. Buybacks, privatizations and mergers all confirm the belief of corporate insiders that bargains still abound.

(3) Be grateful for what you've made so far, because dreadful inflation lies just around the next corner.

This one is so demonstrably silly that it wouldn't be

worth discussing, except for the fact that it seems to be believed—at least every other day—by the hysterics in the bond market. They're terrified by the prospect of any growth other than in their own incomes, and thus they exaggerate all reports of economic improvement. The reality is that America is not likely to have an old-fashioned (or even 1980s-fashioned) boom as long as growth is retarded by three major developments of the 1990s: the sharp tax increases under each of the last two Presidents and the overly-tight monetary policy of a Federal Reserve that comes down with hypochondria every time economic growth pokes its head above 2.5%.

The traders panic with each new set of noise from random commodity prices. The winter was cold and a deal wasn't made with Iraq's oil producers, so oil prices spiked. Rain was scarce in the U.S. heartland, so corn and wheat prices rose. But in the end inflation is a money disease, impure and unsimple, and the Fed just hasn't been printing that much money: enough only to lessen the chance of outright recession in this election year.

(4) Investors act as if stocks will never go down.

Not so. One of the distinguishing factors of this entire bull market has been the way fear routinely checked greed. When a stock group has done brilliantly for a while, there is a tendency to sell it as fervently as it was recently bought. This self-correcting action provides buying opportunities of its own. You may recall, for example, that I wrote in this space last August—before Intel dipped to $25 and Microsoft to just over $20—that I would not be scared away from the technology area by a short-term panic, and that the future of those two bellwether companies "still seems splendid to me."

(5) The next generation of Americans isn't going to live anywhere near as well as its parents.

As I've observed, this same line has been used (with laughable incorrectness) by virtually every generation in the republic's history. We're going through a sluggish patch now, but given the pace of technological and medical progress, the belated streamlining of American industry, and the worldwide move away from socialism and toward free competitive markets, I would make precisely the opposite bet: that the next generation overall will strongly exceed the last in its ultimate economic progress.

(6) The good news has simply gone on too long.

That kind of "we'll have to pay for this" psychology is always persuasive for the guilt-ridden and the constitutionally gloomy, but bull markets do not end on some preordained cycle. They end when the economic underpinnings vanish and/or when popular enthusiasm gets unduly out of hand. Neither condition is yet here.

This doesn't mean the market will now go straight up— I can promise you that it will not—but it does mean that steady, consistent accumulation of quality common stocks still has a long and happy future before it. So ignore the myths and make the money.

From "Will Magellan's Trade Route Run It Aground?"
—June 1996

Gather around, little children, while Uncle Lou confides two of the deepest, darkest secrets of Wall Street that he has uncovered in a lifetime of observation of the financial folks at play. The first secret, which your broker (for obvious reasons) may not wish you to know, is that most small in-and-out traders lose money. Oh, it's fun to try to continually outsmart the market, and it certainly does generate a heap of lovely commissions—not to mention *beaucoup* bucks for Uncle Sam, should he happen to be your favorite charity. But as a sensible means of creating long-term wealth, it ranks just this side of six-deck blackjack.

The second secret may not be so obvious, but it is equally valid—and especially apropos to recent developments in the world of mutual funds. This secret is that most *large* in-and-out traders lose money, too. Nor does perspicacity appear to rise notably when the trades are being made with other people's money.

Investing in mutual funds is supposed to be an excellent way of avoiding the temptation to overtrade. And it certainly *can* be, if you diversify among investing styles and resist the urge to jump ship after a disappointing quarter or two. But the covenant between shareholder and fund manager is supposed to be a two-way pact, and lately that understanding has been violated in some pretty conspicuous places.

The most prominent such case is that of Fidelity Magellan, the nation's biggest mutual fund by a factor of more than two. This past month it was reported that Magellan's three-year return had dropped below that of the S&P 500, for only the second time in two decades. Now, if this were merely an extended case of the market preferring a different category of securities for a time, one could easily counsel patience. After all, Jeff Vinik is a proven money manager with a superb record. But the problem here goes deeper: Vinik stumbled while essentially violating the covenant. In what was supposed to be a long-term-growth fund, he became a short-term trader. And, in keeping with the most profound wisdom of Secret #2, he lost money.

Like the rawest rookie, Vinik ran away when his favorite group fell out of fashion. As recently as last Halloween, technology stocks comprised 45% of Magellan's assets. But when the bears started growling, and these stocks got battered, Vinik failed to do what a money manager of his experience and ability should have done: hang in there and buy more on dips. Instead, he embarked on a slash-and-burn retreat that, by the end of March, had reduced his tech holdings to a mere 3.6%. In other words, Vinik was selling just when he should have been buying—and he was practically out of the market when, inevitably, the severely oversold tech stocks began a spectacular rebound. It was, in short, precisely the kind of mistake one would expect an inexperienced small trader to make.

The mutual-fund universe has room for aggressive-growth funds, in which the manager openly tries to out-smart the crowd with dramatic changes. But that's why we list those funds separately in *Louis Rukeyser's Mutual Funds*, and alert you to both their prospects and their risks. We expect more stability in a fund ostensibly designed for the long-term-growth category. And we expect a fund to be what it purports to be in another sense, too: we expect a stock fund to buy stocks. Yet, as a May report on Magellan's first quarter revealed, Vinik was holding nearly 30% of the fund in bonds (19.2%) and cash (10.1%) as late as March 31—in a year of further stock-market explosions, and a bond decline.

My point is not that Jeff grew too fearful (which he did) or that he made so many bad bets that his fund seriously underperformed most other growth funds (which it did), but that he was proceeding on a path other than the one his shareholders should have expected. If we want an asset-management fund, allocating money to stocks, bonds and cash in accordance with its manager's changing perceptions of the investment outlook, we can choose an asset-management fund. But we should be able reasonably to expect that the manager of a long-term-growth fund will devote his time, and his assets, to picking and investing in stocks. It was that talent that made Magellan so outstanding for so long under Peter Lynch, Morris Smith—and Jeff Vinik. And that is the route on which Magellan should now try to go home.

It is painful to me, professionally and personally, to have to beat up on Jeff Vinik: a good friend and, in my experience with him, a totally decent, honorable and intelligent guy. Indeed, I suspect he would have gotten back on track much faster if Fidelity had not so counterproductively banned him and all their other top people, including even Lynch, from discussing stocks publicly. This has been a throwback to the industry's pervasive close-mouthedness before *Wall $treet Week With Louis Rukeyser* came on the scene in 1970, and it ignores the tremendous advantages that have flowed from a policy of more-open communication with the public. Let's hope Fidelity gets that message soon, for its sake as well as ours.

Nor was Vinik the only manager to lurch wildly off the track that investors had a right to see him pursue; he is merely the most celebrated, which goes with the territory when you run $56.2 billion of other people's money. There is room in this marketplace for all kinds of managers and all kinds of styles, but we ought to know going in which route the portfolio boss intends to follow. We'll then know where to fit him into our own holdings. And when it comes to the long-term-growth portion, I'd just as soon not have an asset allocator or a bond guy—or someone who may not be aware of the dreadful secret that most large in-and-out-traders lose money, too.

From "In This Olympic Summer, Stay Your Course and Win the Gold"
—August 1996

The best news of all this month may be the speed with which pessimism has grown as stock prices have shrunk. Not only have the indexes of adviser and trader sentiment shifted rapidly to dark despair—a wonderful reverse indicator—but even some of the usually stalwart mutual-fund investors have been heading for the exits. A record $4.04 billion was withdrawn from equity funds in the week ended July 17. While in the short run this accelerates the decline, removing the prop that previous cash inflows had provided, it actually strengthens my belief that no enduring cataclysm is at hand. As the ever-astute Laszlo Birinyi reminds us, "Real precipitous declines come about when everybody is happy and confident, not terribly perplexed or concerned." My translation: chew your fingernails all you want (I won't tell), but don't be scared out of a sound investing program because of inevitable, unavoidable, occasional—and ephemeral—paper losses in your portfolio. The bull's not dead, and neither is the American future.

Interestingly, some of the market's shrewdest players seem to think this kind of breather is just what the doctor ordered. For example, exactly one year ago in this commentary, I alerted you that my friend Mike Brown, the "habitually cautious" chief financial officer of Microsoft, had a history of going out of his way to subdue analysts' overly buoyant expectations; he did it again in late July, thereby helping produce a selloff in the face of better-than-expected earnings. Traders are so used to companies overinflating their expectations that they routinely panic in the face of this kind of guidance. (I wouldn't sell my Microsoft—or my Intel—just yet, thank you.) And what seems awful to most investors strikes that master "value" player, Mike Price, as sheer delight. The legendary penny-pincher is actually doing some buying—in the U.S. and abroad.

What's going to happen in the short run? Not a soul knows—including those being most reverently quoted in the financial press. History suggests the likelihood of a "re-test" of the mid-July lows in the averages; if they fail to hold, mindless technicians will rush to sell more— thereby creating even-greater bargains. With computer programs substituting for mature human analysis, extreme intraday volatility is apt to continue. It looks to me like an excellent time for the average investor to ignore the frightening headlines and take a nice relaxing vacation.

My best advice is even simpler: go to the nearest mirror and take a good long hard look at the person staring back at you. Are you really what you said you were a couple of months ago—a serious long-term investor, dedicated to building wealth sensibly and steadily—or are you really a naive scaredy-cat, capable of being flipped helplessly out the kitchen door by the Pundits of Panic every time the market has a selloff, as it did in 1987, 1989, 1990 and 1994? Those who fled at much-lower prices then have been kicking themselves ever since. I believe the same rue awaits those who allow themselves to become terrified in the second half of 1996 by those who would love to convince you that stocks have had it. The reports of the bull's demise have been greatly exaggerated.

From "This Month's Most Valuable Tip Isn't Coming from the Pols"
—September 1996

Well, it's nice to be vindicated so quickly by the extraordinary market rebound after I counseled patience and perseverance amid the bloodbath a month ago, but I'm convinced that there is no value for you in hearing how smart I was yesterday: you want to know what I can do for you today. And only a terminally foolish investor—or an inveterate bear, perennially exploiting the public's perpetual uneasiness about financial risk—casts his or her mind in concrete and refuses to contemplate the possibility of change. So let's reassess where we are right now, and whether it's time to alter our investment strategy.

First, we have an election coming up, as you may already have heard, and that throws a new element of uncertainty into the financial mix. Not, I hasten to add, because of any stereotypical partisan bent in Wall Street; the reality is that there is no meaningful difference over the years in how stocks behave under Democratic or Republican Presidents. Investors focus on vastly more than the party affiliation of the White House incumbent. But there could be passing blips based on policy pronouncements and polls. The bond market, for example, is dramatized in Hollywood legend as the bastion of rock-ribbed Republicans, but in fact it has some important players on the other side, too (where do you think Treasury Secretary Bob Rubin came from?), and its current revulsion against anything that smells of tax cuts and/or faster growth makes it reflexively suspicious of Bob Dole's new economic platform. If Dole should appear in the polls to have a better chance of winning than is now generally thought probable, long-term interest rates could retreat a bit—and stocks could suffer temporary damage as well.

I wouldn't put much enduring importance on this if it happens. In the real world, there is a cavernous gap between what politicians promise while campaigning and what they deliver once elected. Furthermore, a closer study of the Dole tax program reveals that both supporters and critics are exaggerating its likely impact. The vaunted 15% across-the-board tax cut is scheduled to be phased in so slowly, starting next May, that even if enacted the reduction for 1997 would be little more than 3%—and the final effect even in the year 2000 would not repeal the much-denounced Bill Clinton increases in top marginal rates, let alone the 1990 increases under George Bush. (Besides, if you are to believe the rest of the rhetoric, a Dole administration would have totally junked the existing tax code long before then anyhow.) So there's considerably less than meets the eye in the fiscal proposals on both sides of this debate.

Bottom line: temporary jiggles between now and November 5, but nothing likely to change the fundamental outlook. The financial history books are littered with the empty forecasts of those who overpredicted, both in terms of the overall market and individual stocks, as a result of campaign oratory or partisan fervor. Even a Democratic landslide, which might more seriously upset the bond market if it suspected a new spending binge, would take second place to the more basic fact that the economy is moving forward (however grudgingly), with inflation and interest rates continuing to behave remarkably well. So vote with your heart, but invest with your head.

Second, we continue to hear the drumbeat that the market is seriously overvalued—a rataplan that has produced nearly as many phony signals in the past decade as the Elliott Wave (no mean achievement!). I have often detailed my own reasons for disbelieving this all-too-conventional wisdom, and those who followed my advice have made lots of money by conquering this fear. But, again, only a dunce would assume that what was true in the markets yesterday must also be true tomorrow, so let's review the latest evidence there—including what may be the most significant new fact of all.

This new fact helps explain the fallacy behind one of the most frequent complaints of the wrong-way bears: that the prices of stocks, as compared with their dividend yields, are disturbingly high. As I've pointed out in the past, the traditional measures in this area are misleading for a number of reasons. While dividend payouts have been at subnormal percentages as prices skyrocketed, the ability of corporations to pay those dividends has never been more formidable. Managers have chosen to retain a higher-than-previous portion of their income streams. And the operative question for a wise investor should be: what are those companies doing with the money that they could be paying me in dividends?

Now comes word confirming that one of the biggest uses to which those retained earnings have been put is to buy back outstanding shares of the companies' stocks. So momentous is this burgeoning trend that the dollar value of corporate buybacks in the first eight months of 1996— $99.16 billion—has exceeded the total in any previous *full year*. Led by such giant players as Disney, Wells Fargo, IBM, Philip Morris, McDonald's and Chrysler, the titans of American industry are sending a message that, in their informed inside view, the stocks of their companies are still selling too cheap: that they are actually *under*valued. It could be the most valuable stock tip of the month.

Such actions also conform to stockholders' interests in our top-heavy tax system. When a company buys back billions of dollars of its own stock, it does more than boost the value of each share still outstanding (because there are now fewer pieces of the pie, when earnings are divided). It cuts your tax bill. If the buyback increases share prices, U.S. stockholders face only a 28% capital-gains tax when they sell their holdings. Dividends, in contrast, are subject to a top individual federal income tax rate of 39.6%.

Bottom line: some of the nation's shrewdest corporate managers have studied the valuation question and decided that their stocks, under any reasonable long-term perspective, are still excellent buys. And they are putting their money where their mouths are.

In the end, of course, corporate futures depend on how

managers reinvest the rest of their companies' earnings, and whether they stay ahead of the curve by continuing to produce the products and services that customers will buy. And there, there are never any guarantees that yesterday's heroes will also be tomorrow's. But the overall picture, after this reevaluation, seems reassuringly luminous.

From "Standing on the Sidelines Can Be Dangerous, Too"
—October 1996

Most of the genuinely insightful writing that has been done on human beings and the stock market starts with the famous dictum of Socrates: "Know thyself" (a dictum so famous that it has also been attributed to Plato, Pythagoras, Chilo, Thales, Cleobulus, Bias, Solon and the Delphic oracle, among other famous dictors). Socrates, among others, was right.

Plainly, then, the initial analysis you should do if you want to become a successful investor must be of yourself. Are you capable of resisting the comfortable jostle of the crowd? Can you train yourself to develop an intelligent investment program, and then to stick to it when everybody at the neighborhood party tells you you're nuts? Do you really want to make money in the stock market, or do you have some other motivation—a jolly social experience, perhaps, or punishment for your sins elsewhere in this vale?

In other words, the first step in getting your investment act together is taking a good long hard look at the person in the mirror. And nowhere will that search for authentic self-knowledge be more important than in assessing your true tolerance for risk. Two recent events in the world of mutual funds dramatize the perils of not understanding risk.

Say "risk" to the average investor, and he or she will immediately think of the terrible prospect of actually taking a loss. But my point goes well beyond that: the fear of taking a loss can lead, ironically, to even greater risks.

Consider the case of Howard Stein, who retired this past month at the age of 69 after running the Dreyfus Corp. since 1965. Stein, whose powers were greatly diminished after Mellon Bank Corp. bought Dreyfus two years ago, was a classic case of being *too* risk-averse. Dreyfus prospered for a while by concentrating on low-risk bond and money-market funds; indeed, the Dreyfus lion became a symbol of "conservative" investing. But as times changed, and the long-term virtues of equity investing became apparent to multiplying millions of U.S. shareholders over the past 15 years, Dreyfus' failure to adapt to those changes increasingly was perceived as having been one of the major blunders in mutual-fund history. The Dreyfus lion had become a cowardly lion, and was no longer king of anybody's jungle.

Stein now admits he was slow to grasp the growth in equity funds ("I was stupid! I wasn't paying attention!"), and Dreyfus' new CEO, Kip Condron, makes no secret of his intention to give the big cat a more aggressive image. The assets in Dreyfus' stock funds have nearly doubled since Mellon took over the firm, in a $1.8-billion deal, and it has been showcasing such go-go efforts as the Dreyfus Aggressive Value Fund, which was up a nosebleed-inducing 50.34% in this year's first four months. Shed no tears for Howard Stein; his firm may have grown stodgy by failing to encourage sensible risk-taking, but he collected a merger-related payment estimated between $60 million and $100 million, and that can buy a retiree an awful lot of consolation prizes.

So there is more than one kind of risk in investing, and a very real risk is that by pursuing "safety" at all costs, an investor may fail to keep up with the times—or even with inflation. The second recent event referred to above illustrates another peril: that your self-assessment may go out the window the first time trouble appears.

"An investor," say Wall Street cynics, "is merely a disappointed speculator." In other words, people buy in hopes of a quick profit, and if it fails to appear, they simply rationalize that they intended to be long-term holders all the time. Amusing, yes (even if it does give you an uncomfortable shiver of recognition), but that cliché behavior would in fact be more sensible than the all-too-prevalent alternative we saw this summer, when the market took one of its brief, frightening dives. As financial planner Susan Kaplan recalls, "A billion dollars was called out of 401(k) growth funds in July when the market got choppy, and at the end of the month—after growth rebounded—it was put back in." At higher prices, of course.

The bottom line is that a sensible mutual-fund investor should put together a diversified portfolio of funds suited to his or her needs and temperament, with enough "risk" to keep ahead over the longer term—and then not be surprised, let alone panicky, when every fund does not go up every month. There are many ways to construct financial security, but it helps a lot if you start by being a grownup. And as any parent can testify, being a grownup means learning to live with risk.

From "Toss Out the Fruitcakes & Mixed Nuts; Let Reason Rule the Season"

—January 1997

New Year's Resolutions for the winning investor in 1997:

I will never sell on one day's news.

This is one of the most profitable personal trading rules I've developed over the years, and I thought it was high time to share it with you. It applies both to individual stocks and to overall markets. It has saved me a bundle in my own investing, and those who have behaved otherwise have repeatedly paid through the nose—by panicking foolishly at such ephemeral bottoms (and spectacular turnaround points) as those in October 1987 and July 1996. What we've tried to emphasize in our newsletters is a patient, thoughtful approach to assessing the financial future. Such assessments do not change because the market periodically experiences embarrassing bouts of temporary insanity. Let the suckers stampede; for yourself, vow to get a good night's sleep.

I will remember that bearish commentary always sells best—and I will read it with appropriate skepticism.

Extreme pessimism is marvelously marketable, even though I can report to you that in 27 years of *Wall $treet Week With Louis Rukeyser*, indisputably the worst predictions, decade after decade, have come from the perennial gloomsters. Indeed, they all would have disappeared by now (and been forced to seek an honest living) if it were not that most people, frightened by the very thought of investing, are susceptible to those who prey on their fears by suggesting that all will be lost if they persevere. Leading financial magazines and newspapers are often as guilty of this exploitation as many in the direct-mail crowd. So keep your perspective and remember the dreadful batting average of such would-be Cassandras—especially the next time stocks are slumping, and they are screaming that the condition is about to become permanent. I assure you: these nuts will be wrong again.

I will not be buffaloed by the technicians.
Some of my best friends are technical market analysts (or "elves," as I dubbed them long ago), but remember that I'm a very tolerant guy. They are trying diligently to make a science out of what remains an evolving art. Their charts and graphs can be wondrous to behold. But what I have found over the decades is that their predictions can usually be relied on only when tomorrow turns out to be just like yesterday. Forecasting claims to "historical inevitability" have been particularly fallible in recent years, as this unprecedented bull market has unfolded. For all their jargon and impressive software programs, few technicians have spotted the underlying economic changes that produced the actual results of recent years. Instead, the overwhelming majority were "prudent"—and wrong. It was a time for steadiness, not

for fancy in-and-out trading, and somehow that rarely shows up on their charts.

I will not expect to hit a home run every year.

Does any of the above mean that you should now expect your portfolio to return 20%-plus every year from here to eternity? Of course not. Markets get ahead of themselves from time to time, and need a breather—sometimes even (believe it or not) a bear market. But this doesn't change any of the counsel above; in fact, it fortifies it. For while it's easy to stampede for the exits when prices are falling, it's darned near impossible, in the real world, to rush back in at the right time. (We don't pretend in our newsletters to be able to deliver you an unbroken series of investment home runs [nobody ever has, actually], but we do strive to give you the specific ideas and strategy that will keep you hitting well above the average, year after year. It won't be .400 every year, but you'll eventually be in your family's Hall of Fame anyhow.)

I will not let political bias color my economic outlook.

This is a classic error that has seduced folks on both sides of the political equation in the 1990s. Some on the left were led astray by the campaign alarms of 1992 ("The worst economy since the Depression!"); some on the right were fooled into believing that the election of Bill Clinton inevitably meant a return to horrendous inflation. Instead, the economy has continued on a path of slow growth with contained inflation—scarcely euphoria for the average

American seeking higher living standards, but just fine for the financial markets. (And, despite the wild boys of the bond market, who go crazy at least once a fortnight because of their obsession with the ever-misleading "technicals," I expect interest rates—short and long—to continue to behave reasonably well in 1997. There's simply not enough oomph in this economy right now to reach a different conclusion.)

I will keep the faith—and reap its benefits.

Keeping the faith doesn't mean swearing eternally by every stock you own; times change, and so do companies. But keeping the faith means that, the next time stocks are diving and the usual suspects are shouting "Fire!" on Page One, you'll remember that the remarkable restructuring of American industry, with its worldwide competitive dominance, is not about to disappear; that the sobering up of the Baby Boomers, with their sensible turn to greater savings and investment, will not vanish; that a gridlocked government may not delight partisans on either side, but is not likely to go fiscally bonkers, either; that the public musings of would-be National Nanny Alan Greenspan are of less-enduring importance than the Federal Reserve's likely continued benign monetary course; and that a world turning near-universally to capitalism in the 21st Century may actually have learned something from the follies of the 20th.

Have a Happy—and, I hope, another Prosperous—New Year!

From "Alan Speaks and the World Listens—But Our Market Talks Back" —January 1997

We had a riveting example of differing points of view this past month in the reactions at home and abroad to Federal Reserve Chairman Alan Greenspan's murky ruminations about the possibility of "irrational exuberance" inflating the financial markets. In the U.S., once the initial scare was over, prices recovered smartly, as traders (1) recalled that Greenspan, who last spread such gloom in 1993, has throughout his career been a notably-less-than-flawless financial prognosticator, and (2) concluded that with economic numbers as soft as they have been lately, Greenspan was talking a tougher game than he was likely to play. In other words, for all the instant headlines, it was really a non-event. Those who have seen more than a few Fed chairmen come and go realized that a tendency to want to be the National Nanny goes with the job, but what it's really about is not pontificating but putting out a steady, moderate money supply. Not many thrills there, of course, so no wonder Fed chairmen traditionally like to lecture us from time to time; it's a rewarding perk in an underpaid and fundamentally dreary job.

Abroad, however, such grains of salt were conspicuous by their absence. When the man they have come to know as the most powerful central banker in the world goes "tut-tut," it sounds like doom to them. And so, ironically, non-U.S. markets suffered much greater damage than the one about which he was presumably at least vaguely concerned. In Japan, to whose earlier history Greenspan had made allusion (and whose excesses had been infinitely greater, both in stock pricing and in real estate), the Nikkei 225 skidded 2.9% in the next six sessions. In Hong Kong, the Heng Seng Stock Index plunged 5.9%; France's CAC-40 dived 3.9%; and leading exchanges on three continents followed suit. The U.S. market, at its worst, gave back just 2%—and was the first to cheer up. The prophet was most without honor in his own country. Or maybe we just know him better.

Now, let's be fair. There's nothing wrong with being "prudent"—though, since the start of this momentous bull market in 1982, that comforting word has most often been used as an excuse to frighten people away from participating in its bounties. And it's undeniably true that millions of new mutual-fund investors have come on the scene since the Dow Jones industrials have had even what used to be considered a meaningful correction. A Smith Barney survey this past month reported that as many as 40% of fundholders would sell some or all of their holdings if the market fell 15% over a short period of time. They would be foolish to do so (remember, it's supposed to be "*buy* low, *sell* high"), and it's comforting both to see that a little more than half said they would "wait and see" and to remember that fundholders have actually behaved quite sturdily during the occasional sharp selloffs of the 1990s. There's never a law against anyone—even a Fed chairman— reminding you that, in the short run, stocks can go down as well as up. And one of these days, by golly, we'll even have a bear market again. But anyone tempted to the melancholy conclusion that the U.S. stock market's exuberance has become "irrational" is premature at best; prices remain well within the normal range, based on reasonable consensus estimates of 1997 earnings, and the country is likely to continue on its path of slow and relatively noninflationary growth. A market that regularly sells off its high flyers as routinely as this one does may be heading for some setbacks in 1997, but is not apt to plummet into anybody's sub-basement. Even the Fed's.

So relax and enjoy the holidays. You've earned it—and so, I hope, have your investments.

From "This Love Can Last: Hold On Tight To This Sweetheart of a Market"

—February 1997

As the market continues to send spectacular Valentines to those who have given it their committed affection, it may be worth taking a moment to open my heart to you about why I think the love affair with stocks will continue—and why, contrary to so much of what you're hearing lately, the market is actually showing highly rational exuberance. The purpose in doing so is to point you toward even better ways to maximize your profits in 1997.

The general media, and indeed most financial newsletters, have been totally nonplused by this market. My mailbox is still clogged, as yours may be, with apocalyptic screeds from gloomsters who try to scare us into subscribing by preying on our darkest fears and insecurities, predicting Armageddon just around the next corner (or, at the very best, the street after that) and ordering us, with classic idiocy, to "sell all stocks now." For decades now, such absurd counsel has made money only for those who marketed it. People who have been foolish enough to buy it ought to sue for consumer fraud.

As for the nonspecialized media, their coverage of money matters is, alas, only marginally better than it was when I became the economic commentator for ABC News in 1968. But raising the overall grade from F to D– is scarcely a breathtaking achievement in an era when the

American economy has regained world supremacy and when once-scorned concepts of economic freedom are taking over the globe. Just the other day, a television special designed to figure out why the stock market had confounded all the usual suspects leaned so heavily on the conventional "just you wait!" approach that it was advertised with the silliest of all lines about financial matters: "What goes up must come down."

Sorry, guys, but it just ain't so. If it were, the Dow Jones Industrial Average would be making frequent return trips to 41.22, the level it touched the year before I was born. Indeed, the whole story of America (and increasingly the world) is one of long-term improvements in living standards, and to think that the stock market should uniquely ignore this progress is to think like a nervous amateur instead of a successful investor.

A number of readers have been kind enough to remind me of what I wrote in 1995, when I had the temerity to challenge what I called "perhaps the most perennially unchallenged maxim of all": "The most dangerous four words in investing are: 'This time is different.'" I advised then that the real road to financial success was to recognize "not only that this time is indeed different, but that every time is different—and that the most successful investors are those who can adjust to this unorthodox reality."

I repeat this not to crow (there's satisfaction enough in knowing that my stock portfolio has more than doubled since the start of 1995, as I hope yours has), but to advise you to keep your own nerves steady if the market occasionally burps in the next 12 months, and you're tempted to believe that the good news is permanently at an end. Consider what really does move markets, and I think you'll find it easier to keep the faith. Remember that stock prices are at bottom a bet on future earnings. Recent reports have been dominated by pleasant surprises, and therefore the market's vigorous start to 1997 has been anything but irrational. Moreover, in an environment of relatively low and stable inflation and interest rates, such earnings are quite rightly valued more highly than they would be in a more volatile economic era.

Some have been baffled by the stock market's resilience in the face of the recent upward jiggle in rates. They shouldn't be. If rates are rising because the Federal Reserve is tightening and a recession looms, that's bad news for stocks. But if, as in this case, rates are rising simply because of increasing demand for money in a relatively healthy economy, not only is this not fatal for equities but the stock market may well take it as a bullish sign (as it did in early 1996).

I continue to believe that the longer-term trend will produce lower, not higher, bond yields. So I certainly wouldn't sell my own bonds if there is a further hiccup in rates over the next few weeks. Indeed, be ready to take advantage of the slow-learning bond ghouls if they show, once again, their congenital inability to understand that prosperity does not produce inflation; paper-printing governments do. If we're lucky enough to see long-term yields again bounce over 7.25% in the next couple of months, I'll be back in the market buying more bonds—confident that I'm getting a handsome yield, compared with inflation, and that I will also be rewarded with capital gains far sooner than the ghouls expect. I hope you'll join me!

From "Leaving History to the Elves, This Market's Charting Its Own Course"

—March 1997

One of the most frequent questions I've been asked over the years about *Wall $treet Week With Louis Rukeyser* is, "Who are the elves?" The answer is that "elves" is the name I gave many years ago to Wall Street's so-called technical market analysts: the fellows who take a wiggle on a chart, a squiggle on a graph, a strand of witch's hair and a dab of eye of newt, stir it all together with the aid of a proprietary software program, and then announce confidently precisely where every stock you've ever thought of owning will close on March 25, 1999.

Their forecasts are always wondrous to behold—but, alas, rarely accurate. When faced with this disappointing reality, the typical elf has one of two reactions: total denial or a frenetic search for just one more indicator. He or she lives in the demonstrably vain hope that even short-term market action is scientifically predictable, if only one can tweak the chart one more time.

But some people take this sort of thing seriously, and I don't like to argue religion. So we pay obeisance once a week on the television program to this cult, with our very own Elves Index, in which ten indomitable predictors give us their take on where the Dow Jones Industrial Average will be three months from now. (A secret revealed: only half of them are now "pure" technicians—and there's an oxymoron for you!—because the more-devout practition-ers turned out to be so routinely pessimistic, and routinely wrong.) Some weeks, some of them actually get it right.

In our newsletters, we generally stick to other ideas that we've found can more consistently build your wealth—even if they are less likely to produce a gasping reaction akin to reading a supermarket-tabloid headline, to give you a severe coronary, or to induce you to hysterically sell all your stocks every couple of years, at just the wrong time. Call me crazy, but I figure you can watch horror movies on your own time.

The fundamentals (*pace*, elves) remain remarkably strong: slow growth, rising and better-quality earnings, a steady flow of new investment money from aging and wiser Baby Boomers, inflation and interest rates continuing to behave, U.S. industry impressively competitive even with a strengthening dollar. And while we have learned never to exhale while Congress is still in session, there seems a genuine chance at least to move toward lower and more-productive taxation of capital gains. (Yes, this might pro-duce a selloff as people cash in their profits, but in the long run it would improve the return on investment and lead to higher prices.) I wouldn't be thinking of when to exit this market; I would be thinking of seizing opportuni-ties to increase my commitment.

Even if I didn't read it in my chart.

P.S. Don't misunderstand me: some of my best friends are technicians, and I wouldn't even mind if my sister mar-ried one—if his other habits were good (and if I had a sister). As wounded elves often point out, hardly anyone can resist the impulse to become a closet technician once in a while. Some years ago, a devoted technician, who knew (and was astonished) that I'd been making a series of moneymaking calls contrary to his own forecasts, demanded to know what my indicators were. "Well," I said, "there's my pancreas, there's my small intestine and there's the pit of my stomach." I think it made him very unhappy.

From "Another Myth Debunked: Funds Alone Haven't Moved this Market"

—March 1997

Stop the presses: man bites dog.

The customary role of industry trade groups is to convince you—or, better still, your congressman—that there is no occupation more central to the nation's prosperity than the making of widgets, that the national significance of widgetry is infinitely greater than is commonly understood, and that America would sink ignominiously into two oceans if it were not for the overwhelming, impossible-to-overestimate importance of the widget industry. It may seem a bit ridiculous at times, but at least it keeps the lobbyists off the street.

But now comes, of all people, the Investment Company Institute—the trade group for the mutual-fund industry—to tell us that the importance of mutual funds has been vastly overrated in the 1990s. It's as if the steel industry had said, "Heck, don't pay so much attention to *us*; we don't matter nearly as much as you think, and after all, the customers can always buy aluminum."

Specifically, the Investment Company Institute's chairman, Don Powell, scoffed outright at the widespread notion that the country's growing affection for mutual-fund investing has been the central power behind the great bull market of the 1990s. This belief is espoused both by those who approve of the massive new inflows of cash and by those who regard it as an ominous sign that the whole Wall Street mountain must soon crumble because of the new dominance of these crass amateur investors.

"It's hard to make the case that mutual-fund inflows are making stocks go up," said the heretical ICI chairman. When you get right down to it, he declared, their presence in the overall market is still relatively small—they held just 14% of U.S. stocks last year—and it seemed obvious to him that the billions of dollars so famously pouring into stock funds could not possibly be the main engine behind the market's surge.

Then his chief economist, John Rea, piled on the self-deprecating heap, mocking the conviction that the market will have to keep going up because so many investors are discovering mutual funds. As Rea seemed to see it, you had to be nuts to surmise that there was much correlation between fund inflows and stock prices. While it was true that a net $175.7 billion went into stock funds last year and the S&P 500 duly rose 23%, considerably less money ($116.5 billion) had bolstered the funds in 1995—when the S&P returned 34%. Stock price movements are determined not by money flows, Rea asserted, but by earnings growth and interest rates.

Well, what do you know? In Wall Street's great chicken-and-egg debate, it may be rising prices that are drawing mutual-fund investments, rather than vice versa.

While it's never pleasant to be told that you and I are less overwhelmingly important than we might previously have believed, I'm convinced that—up to a point—the

ICI's skepticism about the influence of its own industry is justified. But don't assume from this that the authentic behemoth is the self-important institutional investors, like banks, pension funds and insurance companies. For though it may be disconcerting to learn that mutual funds own only about a seventh of all stocks, it turns out that the largest single bloc of shareowners is individual holders of stock. Despite the tremendous impact of institutions on the ever-volatile daily trading, individuals still own 48% of the total. Add to that the 14% held by mutual funds, and you can see that we peons are considerably less insignificant in the marketplace than you might guess from the haughtiness of the fat cats.

Truth is, owning mutual funds does not have to be an either-or choice, and many successful investors divide their holdings between funds and individual stocks. And while 14% may not sound like a lot, the growing enthusiasm of newcomers to equity investing has captured the attention of the politicians—whose constitutional inability to perform simple arithmetic is somehow magically cured when they are faced with the task of counting votes. This means that fund investors may not only affect stock prices at the margin, but may quite centrally affect government policy. The prospect of actually getting a cut in the capital-gains tax this year has been helped unmistakably by the growing numbers of middle-class taxpayers who have been investing successfully in mutual funds. These voters have become painfully aware that when politicians fatuously attempt to justify counterproductive, investment-slowing revenue measures as "soaking the rich," they now mean you and me.

So, it transpires, we fund investors are not wholly insignificant, either. We have helped the market, we have helped the country—and we have helped ourselves. Maybe the authentic meaning is that we don't really need the lobbyists that much, either.

From "Don't Let a Temporary Tumble Turn You Into an April Fool"
—April 1997

It's every woman's lament. "You guys," she will say with a sigh (sometimes even an affectionate one), "are so predictable."

What else are we to make of a stock market that this year proved its eternal fickleness by transforming technology stocks from the group it adored without reservation to the group it loved to hate, in less time than it takes to plan a decent wedding?

What else are we to make of financial markets that, faced with the possibility of a mild corrective tightening by the Federal Reserve, immediately assumed that inflation was rampaging and/or that a heedless Fed was about to repeat the embarrassing overkill that butchered bonds in 1994?

And, indeed, what else are we to make of a smug bunch of Wall Street hotshots who, when they're not expressing unwarranted contempt for their emotional and financial betters—the small individual investors—routinely stampede like frightened zebras en route across the Serengeti?

You guys are so predictable.

The clear job of the rest of us, at frenetic times like these, is to resist the temptation to enlist in the panic platoons ourselves—and to see if, as is so often the case, the hysteria of the institutional investors is once again providing us with opportunities to remain calm and make profits at their expense.

Let's begin with a look at the authentic economic background. There has been, by anyone's reckoning, a little more bounce than predicted to the early-1997 U.S. economy. It is by no means clear, however, that this is a permanent reversal. For much of the winter over much of the U.S., temperatures were unusually benign—and this helped juice the numbers in areas ranging from construction to retail sales. To some extent, the winter's gains could be the rest of the year's losses. While there are finally signs of some strengthening in workers' wages (and a good thing, too, most Americans probably feel), we're not about to turn national anemia into national boom: this remains the weakest economic recovery since World War II.

A closer examination of the latest inflation numbers underlines the conclusion that Wall Street got too spooked too fast. For the first two months of 1997, consumer prices actually rose at a piddling 2.3% annual rate, well down even from last year's opening-two-month pace of 4%. And if you pay closer attention, as the Fed does, to the "core" rate (which excludes the ever-volatile food and energy prices), you get an even-lower annual rate of 2.2% for January and February 1997. For years, as such impressively low numbers persisted, the frustrated inflation hawks have been warning, in exasperation, "Just you wait!" It looks as if they're going to have to continue that lament for a while longer.

All of which suggests to me that, as I've been telling you for some time, long-term bond yields are fundamentally too high and provide an interesting opportunity both for investors and traders. Despite the headlines, yields have not yet gotten as high as they did when we established our last positions in mid-1996, but I would certainly not sell at these levels—and, as previously advised, would be getting ready to add to my positions if long-term Treasury yields poke above 7.25%.

Stocks could again surprise on the upside if interest rates do fall and earnings come in a bit healthier than are anticipated. But when you compare bond yields around 7% with inflation around 2% (and possibly overstated, as economists of all stripes are coming to believe), you can see that the ever-delirious bond ghouls—who have not yet learned that growth and inflation are not inseparable—are once again selling bonds down close to giveaway levels. In the classic Rothschild tradition, let's be accommodating: if everybody wants to sell bonds, let's get ready to buy a few.

As for the slaughter in the technology sector, this would justify the conclusion with which we started— "You guys are so predictable"—all by itself. It wouldn't be a year in mid-1990s Wall Street if we didn't have a technology massacre along the way. Indeed, the stocks often seem victims of their own inventions, which so unnervingly speed up and exaggerate movements in both directions.

At least once a year, I find myself writing reassuring words in this commentary for scared-to-death technology investors, and plainly 1997 is not destined to be an exception. The latest bloodbath was produced, not unusually, by a combination of fundamental and hortatory factors. On the fundamental side, traders reacted in horror to some less-than-wonderful numbers, notably in the computer-networking area, and on the hortatory side, silly reporters gave excessive exposure to perennial technology bears who in the real world have been dreadfully, conspicuously wrong for years.

This is not to say that every technology stock will go to the skies every month. The area is notoriously volatile, given to sudden surges of enthusiasm and debilitating bouts of despondency. But, sure enough, the selloff was barely under way before we heard that old and foolish Wall Street yell, "Technology is dead!" You betcha. As I have noted in similar past periods, technology is not dead unless the future is dead. And, as is their wont, the manic sellers threw out the gold with the rust.

From "Hot Shots Step Aside: The Little Guys (& Gals) Are Here to Stay" —April 1997

When the going gets tough, the smart relax. That's the best antidote to the kind of hysteria that has been gripping the stock market lately, notably in the roller-coaster technology sector, and the good news is that mutual-fund investors continue to demonstrate a greater degree of intelligence, perseverance and downright maturity in this regard than the lofty behemoths of Wall Street.

Hark, for starters, to the ever-incisive words of Mike Holland. After a brilliant career in the world of big, *big*, BIG money, Mike is convinced that the much-scorned little guys are, year in and year out, the market's authentic reservoir of "common sense and reason." And his own attractively simple investment techniques, used with conspicuous initial success in his Holland Balanced Fund, intentionally eschew such routine trappings of the modern institutional world as complicated computerized formulas and push-button sell programs. Mike prefers what he calls, with characteristic good humor, the commonsensical "stomach test."

Now, in further support of my belief that the wisdom of the typical small investor is profoundly underrated in Wall Street, comes a new study commissioned by Nasdaq. Much of what it tells us merely confirms (albeit strikingly) the unprecedented explosion of interest in finance generally, and mutual funds in particular: in 1990, 13% of American adults owned funds; today, it's a whopping 40%.

Stock ownership among adult Americans has doubled, to 43%. And where 60% of investors included funds in their portfolios seven years ago, now it's 88%. Huge numbers, indeed; but we all kind of knew that.

What may startle the skeptics—who continue, every time the market hiccups, to issue jeremiads foretelling panicky flight by inexperienced know-nothings—is the impressive evidence that most individual investors actually have their eyes open and are in the market for the long haul. Nearly nine out of 10 intend to use their holdings for retirement. A majority say that a major move downward in stocks would not cause them to change their investment plans. And, in a dramatic shift since 1990, the number who say they're counting on outside sources such as a pension or Social Security as their main source of retirement money (rather than their own savings and investments) has tumbled from 49% to 29%. Little boys and girls are not as easy to fool as they used to be.

Speaking of which, those "little guys" increasingly *are* female: 47% of all U.S. investors, up from 37% in 1990. Of those women, 45% said they were the primary decision-makers in their households regarding investments. (The other 55% presumably were being discreet.) History tells us that women as a group tend to be more-conservative, less-impetuous investors, and that augurs well for the long haul, too. Two final figures further confound the outmoded stereotype of investors as old, male and elitist: most are in fact under 50, and fully half never graduated from college. The people's capitalism has arrived.

From "As the Bears Pitch the Blues, Let's Swing for the Fences"
—May 1997

Back in the dark Depression era, people who were feeling totally miserable about their lives and futures made a cult classic of a particularly depressing dirge called "Gloomy Sunday," also known as "The Hungarian Suicide Song," and sung at its most moving, as so many tunes were, by the unforgettable Billie Holiday. So disheartening was its impact that the song was said to have been widely banned, lest it drive hordes of listeners entirely over the edge.

Well, I always thought the magnificent and doomed Ms. Holiday was one of the century's greatest musical artists, but I never regarded her as an expert on investments. Her searing rendition came to mind this past month, however, as I read through some of the downbeat comments that flooded my newspapers, television screen and mailbox—and maybe yours, too—in the wake of what has so far turned out to be an entirely modest midcourse correction, sending the Dow Jones Industrial Average down precisely 9.8% from its all-time high. All we needed to complete the mournful spectacle was to have Lady Day sing the blues.

We all know that fear sells, especially in times of crisis—indeed, much of the less-reputable financial "information" sector seems to have that as its permanent motto. So I wasn't surprised to see all the usual suspects scurrying out of the woodwork, not to confess that their frightening counsel has been perennially, ludicrously wrong (be serious, man), but to assure us that all the other worms had finally turned in their direction. The bull market was over, they shrieked; the only remaining issue was whether the next few weeks would be (a) 1987; (b) 1929; or (c) Armageddon.

You betcha. While the market's patterns have always seemed to me less baffling than customarily described (they are hysterically erratic in the short term, but ultimately rational in the long), this past month was one of those rare occasions when I felt I could spot the exact moment that recovery was at hand. It came in a Bloomberg story April 9 reporting that the number of U.S. advisers who expected stocks to rally had fallen to the lowest level in 18 months. Could it be possible that all those wrong-way Corrigans were actually tossing such a half-speed pitch right down the middle of the plate for us? Thank you, guys! Your generosity may be unintentional, but it is certainly unfailing. As if that weren't enough, the same article told of a Quick & Reilly poll that found the most bearish investment sentiment in at least five years. Clearly, they actually *were* ringing a bell at the bottom this time!

Within two days, the Dow had bottomed, closing at 6391.69, and the startling turnaround astonished every pessimist in the pasture. The following week produced the biggest weekly percentage gain for the Dow since 1991— and the biggest weekly *point* gain ever (311.86)—and, as if to rub it in, the week after *that* produced the best *daily* percentage gain since 1991. I suppose you and I should be grateful for the avalanche of gloom that made it possible for the market so quickly to validate the headline on last month's issue: "Don't Let a Temporary Tumble Turn You Into an April Fool."

From "Basking in Green Under the Rockets' Red Glare"
—July 1997

There is an old theory in pop psychiatry that most gamblers want to lose. The notion is that people are either so uncomfortable with their material success or so embarrassed about their personal behavior that they unconsciously want to assuage their guilt by "giving something back."

I've never been fully convinced by this argument—nor, I suspect, would it seem especially plausible to a black-jack player hoping fervently for the dealer to bust, or a craps shooter praying that the dice will honor him with one more four the hard way. But I must confess that an astonishing number of stock-market investors seem to be rooting subliminally for their own failures.

How else can you explain their inability, in many cases stretching over the past 15 years, to recognize and partici-pate fully in what continues to be the greatest bull market of our lives? Why, with the Dow now having reached lev-els fully 10 times where it was in 1982, does there contin-ue to be such a willing market of suckers for charlatans peddling the argument that the end of the world is nigh? Just last summer, one overpublicized guru frightened tens of thousands into buying a new newsletter whose blood-curdling advice was: "Sell all stocks now!" Another long-time Wrong Way Corrigan is still (apparently profitably) mailing old, already-discredited material that predicted

1997 would be a year of "devastated" investments, higher inflation and a steep rise in the price of gold. You betcha.

These bum steers succeed because most people are scared to death about money, and therefore vulnerable to the fear-mongering prophets of doom—no matter how much this has cost the Nervous Nellies in profits of the more satisfying kind. I'm proud that we have been conspicuously on the other side of this forecasting game, not just telling you each year that the bull market had much further to go but also counseling you not to panic, along with most of the media, when passing squalls rained fleetingly on your parade. Our April 1997 headline, you may recall, was "Don't Let a Temporary Tumble Turn You Into an April Fool," while in May we got even stronger: "As the Bears Pitch the Blues, Let's Swing for the Fences." As you know, the market proceeded to explode anew, in highly spectacular fashion, and I keep reading elsewhere that nobody saw it coming. Uh-huh.

But, as I've often noted, you don't want to hear how smart we were yesterday; you want to know what we can do for you today. And so, let's focus for a moment on how you might slightly alter your investment posture this month to take advantage of the changes likely to be around the next financial bend.

First, I would substantially maintain my overall position. There are, to be sure, occasional hints that sectors of the market are getting tired. Mighty Intel suggested there might be one minor quarterly disappointment, in a period of product transition, and the ever-volatile technology area went into red alert; other fine performers, such as Oracle, were punished simply for reporting earnings that were precisely in line with estimates—thereby suggesting that the best way to succeed with some of today's nutty analysts is to lie to them in advance. If the squall gets more serious in this sector, I would regard it as still-another gift to sensible long-term investors—a time to buy, and certainly not a time to sell.

Avoid the temptation, which has turned so many gurus into goats, of trying to be too cute and time this market. In the high-speed computer age, violent movements that used to last months are often over (and reversed) within days or even hours. Winners will continue to stay with the trend, which remains: up, up, up. And not because of "irrational exuberance," about which Alan Greenspan mused so memorably (and so incorrectly) early last December—since when, the Dow has risen by nearly a quarter. Listen to Alan for other reasons if you wish, but for heaven's sake don't look to him for stock-market advice.

From "In Wall Street's Pennant Race, Fear Strikes Out"
—September 1997

Fear and greed, greed and fear. We're not talking Greek tragedy here (though on some days recently, you could be forgiven for thinking we were), but the traditional analysis of the intense, competing emotions that send financial markets reeling, apparently irrationally, in one direction or the other. What I want to suggest to you this month is that, contrary to the conventional media conclusion, much the stronger of those two drives is fear—and that understanding this counterintuitive reality may help you make a lot more money with your own investments in the years ahead.

I was reminded of this in a very human way when I received a nice letter from a young woman in Denville, N.J. (whose name I will not reveal, for reasons of mercy) right after the Dow Jones Industrial Average tumbled 247.37 points on August 14—and the inveterate gloomsters of Wall Street and journalism were once again shrieking that the bull market had collapsed. Just a week before, she related, her father had given her a gift of money and suggested she invest it all. She had resisted, she proudly told me, because she feared "a repeat of 1929." And now, she said, she had been vindicated; the "rainy day" had arrived, it clearly wasn't "only a correction" and "I think I was right."

It's always tough, though it happens quite frequently, when somebody writes me a letter full of dire predictions about the stock market that have already been proved false by the time the Postal Service gets around to delivering the writer's forecast. And by the time I got this letter, the Dow had already regained all it had lost on that discomfiting Friday, and then some. This is, of course, no guarantee that stocks won't go lower in the months ahead—scary volatility is the market's way of keeping the crowd from making too many profits—but it does provide a hint of the excessive power of fear. Life without risk is an academic fantasy, and as we have seen again and again, the greatest risk most people take in investing is not taking enough of what they initially perceive to be risk.

I don't want to beat up on the young lady—especially since she said she and her Dad were "big fans" who "still plan our 'quality time' together so we can watch *Wall $treet Week With Louis Rukeyser* on Friday nights." (A saintly family tradition that will surely eventually bring her both infinite wisdom and fabulous wealth.) Plainly, she was the victim not just of her own natural trepidation about money matters, but of the entirely predictable hysteria that immediately infected the airwaves and public prints after a week that saw a 4% slide in the Dow, exacerbated by extensive program trading of expiring stock and index options, following a spectacular advance of 30% in less than four months. If that's an authentic disaster, I'm Clark Gable.

Anyone wanting further evidence that fear is actually a much more powerful force than greed in the financial markets might also consider the following:

(1) Though the market historically heads higher on two days out of three, and has done even better of late, the days it goes down are usually much more dramatic than the days it goes up.

The worst daily point drop ever recorded by the Dow was 508.00 points on October 19, 1987. The best daily point gain ever recorded by the Dow was 186.84 points two days later. Not only is that best daily gain little more than a third as large as the worst daily drop, but it would rank no higher than fifth on the list of the Dow's biggest daily swings. There were, indeed, two days of larger point losses this summer alone, and another in 1989. Every one of them terrified most investors, and produced panicky coverage in the media. Not a one of them turned out to mean a darned thing in the broad sweep of investment history.

(2) Excessive pessimism about the financial markets is routinely peddled by two classes of would-be experts: those who know they're conning you and those who don't.

In the first category are the conscienceless charlatans who know that most people are always scared to death about money and are therefore always susceptible to terrifying forecasts and apocalyptic advice. These perennial losers (for your account, not necessarily for theirs) are not really in the financial-advice business at all; they're in the mail-order business. Having located a constituency that wants to have its darkest fears confirmed, they provide that service on a regular basis.

The second category includes reporters who, in a notoriously ill-paid profession (and this is the voice of experience talking!), usually have little meaningful experience in the financial markets, tend to regard them as appendages of what they see as a class-war economic system, feel that anybody who makes more money than they do must be a scam artist, and are inclined to believe any idiot who comes along and says that the average guy is being set up for a swindle. That's why you see the same old suspects habitually quoted in the major media, even if they haven't called any market right in a generation. And that's why, for example, the down days typically get much more imposing coverage on Page 1 than the up days, even in a historic bull market like this one. (The *New York Times* has so often erroneously discerned a "sea change" in recent years that by now every investor in America should be at least 20,000 leagues under the sea.)

For both these categories, fear sells. But it doesn't put any bread on *your* table.

(3) If greed were the more powerful emotion, this bull market would be missing one of its most important props: the violence with which it periodically corrects.

It's extraordinarily healthy that the market has these steep turnarounds from time to time. Sometimes stocks do get ahead of themselves. (When Coca-Cola peaked on June 16, its price/earnings ratio had skyrocketed to 43 times its predicted 1997 profits.) And one of the most encouraging features of this phenomenal bull movement has been its willingness regularly to sell off specific stocks, industry groups and the market itself in a self-correcting cleansing mechanism, forming the basis for continued ascents to unpredicted heights. It's one of the important reasons I see scant evidence, even now, that excessive greed has sent the market to levels it cannot, over the long haul, maintain and elevate.

None of the above is intended to assure you that the market will never give you another fright. Quite the contrary: that is its stock in trade (and its trade in stocks). But the basic reasons for optimism over any reasonable long-term perspective remain resolutely in place: memorably low inflation (consumer prices are quieter than they have been in more than a decade, and producer prices have posted a string of monthly declines unmatched since Herbert Hoover was President); tame interest rates (as the Federal Reserve has just confirmed); relative industrial peace (despite the talk of a fired-up union movement following the UPS strike, labor costs have actually slowed this year); and an economy that is clearly moderating but not expiring.

From "Case Closed: Investors Tell Greedy Funds, 'We Object!'"
—September 1997

Even in this greatest of all bull markets, not every mutual-fund investor is wearing a big smile these days, and for many of the disappointed it has been an open-and-closed case. Thereon hangs a tale of industry greed vs. consumer interests that deserves a wider ventilation.

The typical mutual fund is what the industry calls "open end," which simply means that the management company will sell as many shares as the public is willing to buy— and will redeem those shares on any given day for whatever their proportional holdings are worth (the shares' "net asset value"). But there's another category— "closed-end" funds—that operates quite differently. With a closed-end fund, the company issues only a set number of shares, and these shares then trade like stocks, usually on a major exchange. If you own a closed-end fund and want to sell, you won't get the net asset value; you'll get whatever a buyer is willing to pay. If that's more than the net asset value, the fund is said to be selling at a premium; if less, it's a discount.

Historically, that wasn't necessarily considered to be a bad deal. Early in this century, most mutual funds were closed end, and if one of them sold at a discount to its net asset value, holders were assured that this was a terrific advantage: they were, in effect, buying dollars for only 90 cents, and eventually the discount might disappear or even transmogrify into a premium. Indeed, such changes were not uncommon, and the beauty part was that they often seemed to bear no relationship to any logical cause—a sort of unexpected jackpot for the patient.

Lately, though, the closed-end scene has been considerably less pretty. Lingering discounts became the mode, and shareholders grew understandably restive. The suspicion grew that, at worst, many funds were failing to live up to their prospectuses, and that even at best, many fund managers and boards were systematically putting their own interests ahead of those of their shareholders. Agitation built for converting such funds to open-end status, which would of course result in an immediate increase in selling price—since the discounts would vanish and shareholders could redeem their holdings at their (higher) net asset value.

Since many managers also hold shares, you might ask, why should they resist a conversion that would benefit their own holdings as well? The answer lies not in the way they resemble outside shareholders, but in the fees they collect from managing other people's money. When made whole by a conversion from closed-end to open-end status, many shareholders simply take the money and run. Typically, one-third to one-half of the assets will leave the fund. And the management fee will suffer a similar reduction.

But shareholders are not as easy to push around as they used to be, and proposals to convert funds are at record levels. Some funds are responding; at least 10 have either converted or liquidated this year, and eight more have scheduled shareholder votes. Meanwhile, the Securities and Exchange Commission has warned the closed-end industry to make sure its shareholders are getting their money's worth. As closed-end fund expert Thomas J. Herzfeld puts it, "The momentum has definitely shifted in shareholders' favor." Not coincidentally, the average discount on closed-end funds has been shrinking: from 10.2% in late 1995 to 8% in mid-1996 to 5.9% now.

Still, wary investors are scarcely growing enamored of the breed. Only one new closed-end stock fund was launched in the first half of 1997. It's the Dessauer Global Equity Fund, managed by my friend and television panelist John Dessauer. And since John is nobody's fool, his fund was deliberately set up in a highly unusual way— unlike any other U.S. closed-end fund—to meet legitimate investor concerns about this class of investments. If, after its first 18 months of operation, his fund trades on the New York Stock Exchange at a discount of 5% or more for 15 straight days, it will automatically convert to an open-end fund—unless 80% of the holders vote to keep the closed-end status. Not surprisingly, investors liked this provision a lot, and immediately started trading Dessauer Global Equity at a premium to its net asset value.

Open *minds* can be nice for shareholders, too.

Mutual Musings: Well, it's happened again: you've outsmarted the alleged pros. When the Dow Jones Industrial Average climaxed a swift 565-point (7%) decline with a 247.37-point (3.1%) plunge on a single day, August 15, the institutional-investment world and the media that venerate it were chock-full of panicky reactions. Our comeuppance was here at last, they believed, and which exit should we head for now?

Contrast that predictable instant hysteria with the behavior of the typical mutual-fund investor. He or she shrugged, and figured that such occasional shocks were the price you pay for a sensible long-term investment program. The volume of telephone calls was close to normal at Fidelity Investments, Vanguard Group and T. Rowe Price Associates. Vanguard said "it appears that investors are staying the course," and Fidelity reported that while a small minority of investors did move assets into money-market funds, the vast majority wisely did nothing.

It would be pleasant to think that the market's instant snapback the following week caused at least a few red faces in the Panic Platoon, not to mention its allies who wrote all those terrifying front-page headlines. Pleasant, but improbable. For years now, I've been reporting that the much-maligned individual shareholder has been showing far more patience, maturity and financial acumen than the bulk of the stratospherically compensated money managers who disdain him or her. It hasn't been generally recognized yet, but meanwhile we have our profits to console us.

From "At Wall Street's Thanksgiving, What's Past Could Be Turkey" —November 1997

The customary criticism of us Americans is that we have no memory, and it is a true and grievous fault, though historically it has made it easier for us to adapt to new friendships with old enemies, from England to Russia. Contrast that with the ever-simmering antagonisms of, say, the Balkans and the Middle East, where forgetting any slight of the past three millennia is regarded as high treason, and America's inability to hold a grudge for more than 13 seconds straight begins to look a little less deplorable.

It even turns out to be helpful in investing once in a while. This is counterintuitive, because we all have been soberly instructed since our schooldays to remember the words of George Santayana: "Those who cannot remember the past are condemned to repeat it." Santayana was born in Spain; his contemporary, Henry Ford, the quintessential American optimist, thought that "history is more or less bunk." When it comes to the financial world, the truth is somewhere in between. It's useful to have some sense of what came before, of course, but it can be extremely costly to become a prisoner of that past.

The temptation to succumb to that imprisonment is a conspicuous feature of both the financial and economic worlds this remarkable autumn, so let's take a moment to analyze it and see if it can provide clues to our own moneymaking activities in 1998 and beyond.

Financially, the ubiquitous reprises of the so-called Crash of 1987, on the tenth anniversary of an event that turned out to have far less meaning than was first so widely assumed, remind us of what we might call the perils of pessimistic parallels. I remember one prominent captive of the wave-and-cycle nonsense who told me condescendingly at the time how ignorant I was not to realize that a market selloff of that size *always* had to mean, at best, a horrendous recession, and at worst, a cataclysm that would make the 1930s look like a tea party. Uh-huh. In retrospect, he was just a particularly foolish exponent of the same fallacy that has led the overwhelming majority of market "timers" repeatedly astray in the intervening decade. Most "technical analysis" founders whenever tomorrow fails to check in as an exact duplicate of yesterday. Which it peskily keeps on refusing to do.

Similarly, the economic argument of the season is over whether this really is a "New Economy" or a "New Order" or a "New Era" or a "New Paradigm" —or some other version of what has become, as it were, the daily "news." Chairman Alan Greenspan of the Federal Reserve has been conducting a fascinating public debate on this subject, taking alternate sides on alternate days, like a carparker in New York City. (If Greenspan confuses you, don't despair: that was precisely his intention.) And while this might seem like one more academic debate among economists as to exactly how many jobless claims can dance on the head of a pin, it provides a key to understanding why the greatest bull market of our lives is not over yet. It also helps us comprehend why some of Wall Street's favorite clichés, from "what goes up must come down" to "trees don't grow to the skies" to "the most dangerous four words in investing are: 'this time it's different'" have frightened investors away from full participation in this historic market, rather than guiding them to its maximum profits.

For myself, I'm instinctively wary of such facile phrases as "New Era," which can too easily stir memories of failed pronouncements of the past. But I think it's important for anyone who wants to be a successful investor to recognize, as so many have refused (to their cost) to recognize in recent years, that some things really have changed out there. Let me recall for you two sentences that I wrote in the December 1995 issue of *Louis Rukeyser's Wall Street*, long before the current debate about "New Paradigms" was all around us: "This month, as we contemplate a nervous market and plot a strategy for how to deal with it, I want to begin by boldly challenging the previously unchallengeable. My thesis for you today is not only that this time is indeed different, but that every time is different—and that the most successful investors are those who can adjust to this unorthodox reality."

That approach has made us a lot of money in the intervening two years. It recognized that the explosion of freer markets across the globe has created different conditions: providing more consumers, holding down wage demands, intensifying competitive pressures on management to restructure, demanding a more rapid pace of product improvement. In turn, the historic boom in high technology—which moved so fast that governments didn't have time to "help" us use it—made formerly elusive productivity enhancements available to virtually every business on the planet. (Everything improved except the government's statistical tools for measuring it.) Under these changed conditions, with corporations able to manage inventories better and respond more agilely to changing market conditions, the old rules of inevitable cyclicality and reinflation must be altered to make any sense of what's really going on. I don't think anyone has managed yet permanently to repeal the business cycle, but I suspect that the old bugaboo of inflation is less a problem now than the new danger that excessive monetary tightness, by central bankers persisting in fighting the last war, could produce its opposite: global deflation, with more goods than customers.

From "Guard Your $: More Funds Trying to Lock and Load"
—November 1997

A young money manager once told me that he had had a disillusioning meeting with my old friend and certified global-investing immortal, John Templeton. Since John is normally among the most upbeat and inspiring personages of the Twentieth Century, I wanted to know what had gone wrong. "Well," said the young money manager, "I told him that I had a new mutual fund, and asked for his advice on how to make it succeed. He immediately replied, 'Get brokers.' 'But, sir,' I said, 'mine is a no-load fund.' Templeton was undeterred. 'Get brokers,' he repeated, and walked on."

Well, John, I suspect, was just trying to be characteristically kind, based on his own long experience in mutual-fund management and marketing. After all, through most of his career, the favored cliché in the industry was that "mutual funds are sold, not bought." The idea was that people had to be talked into making this kind of purchase—or, to put it more gently, had to receive the kind of expert advice and guidance that they simply couldn't get anywhere else. The resident geniuses in brokerage offices would hold your hand and direct your purchases, and in return for this incomparable service they were surely entitled to a substantial sales commission, euphemistically referred to as a "load."

In fact, when we began *Wall $treet Week With Louis*

Rukeyser in 1970, loads of up to 8.5% were common in the industry. And many brokers regarded me as a dangerous radical when I wrote unequivocally in 1974 in my first book, *How to Make Money in Wall Street*: "Buy a 'no-load' fund." That advice alone narrowed your choice impressively, since fully nine out of ten mutual funds then came with loads attached. Since then, of course, the no-load segment of the industry has exploded, as more and more investors discovered that they were often overpaying for broker advice—and that it was usually better to start with all your dollars working for you, rather than having several percentage points peeled off the top before the money manager even began to strut his stuff.

Ominously, as I write this, the trend may be reversing. And it's something for you to keep a wary eye on as you plan your own future investments. Before detailing this threat of a counterrevolution by the load collectors, let me say that I'm not a purist about this. When you get a genuine investment genius like Templeton, the sales charge can become unimportant as years of happy returns ensue. But my own preference is for funds whose sales charges are 3% or lower (in my book, zero is best!). There is no evidence that load-fund managers, on balance, do better than no-load managers, so why not have all your cash working for your own account?

Every once in a while, a manager comes along who seems compellingly superior to his peers, even after you pay a load. For most fund investing most of the time, however, you're much better off putting your money into a selection of no-load (or, at worst, low-load) offerings. Doing just that has been the sensible trend of most of the last generation.

Now, however, come some worrisome straws in the common-sense wind. For the past five years, as new and inexperienced investors have flooded into the fund market, the direct-sales channel (usually via an 800 number) has been losing market share. And fund executives, eager not to let a single dollar escape their coffers, have been paying attention. In mid-October, for example, Chicago-based Stein Roe & Farnham said it was moving for the first time in its 65-year history to sell funds to investors through "full service" brokers, rather than marketing them directly with no extra sales fees. As part of the change, and presumably as a sop to the brokers, the company said it would no longer directly market its venerable, $625-million Stein Roe Growth Fund to individual investors who don't already own shares in it. Since this fund has been a solid performer, with a three-year annualized return of 29.41%, this was a disturbing step. A Stein Roe spokesperson hastened to say that the firm was "not planning to close any more of our 'no-load' mutual funds," conceding that closing this one had been "a requirement to making an entry into the intermediary market." (Translation: the brokers made us do it.)

Unfortunately, the backtracking by Stein Roe is not an isolated case. Kansas City's American Century Cos., which sold nothing but no-load funds until late last year, said in October that it is issuing new classes of shares for an additional 19 funds that will be marketed by financial advisers to investors. This gives the firm 38 funds that now charge at least some marketing fees.

Ironically, one of the important recent innovations that made it possible for the average investor to trade no-load funds with ease has become a catalyst for the counter-trend. It's the availability of one-stop shopping for funds at discount houses like Charles Schwab or AccuTrade. The same convenience that makes it simpler for you to buy and sell a variety of no-load funds is also there for brokers and other financial advisers who charge a fee. Before, such advisers were limited because of the operational difficulties in managing complex fund portfolios. Today, fee-based financial advisers in the U.S. control an estimated $370 billion in assets, including about $75 billion invested in mutual funds. (Comparable figures five years ago: $120 billion and $10 billion.)

The alleged *raison d'être* in charging for what used to be given away free is that the average fund investor is confused by the vast number of funds now available, and needs to pay for help. That may be true for the "average," but it shouldn't be true for you. Around here, we represent the customer, not the industry pooh-bahs.

From "Why Wall Street's Analysts So Often Get It Wrong"
—January 1998

When I last lunched privately with Alan Greenspan, the Federal Reserve chairman confided that even he had trouble figuring out the press. The media coverage of his remarks, he said, regularly surprised him: he never knew when reporters were going to overreact, or in which direction. He would make what he regarded as routine restatements, and suddenly they would be trumpeted as major news.

This past month, I had some personal experience of what Alan was talking about. And not for the first time. Nearly three decades ago, for example, while I was serving as ABC-TV's economic commentator, I correctly forecast a mild recession, and was startled to find this measured pronouncement splashed as front-page news in West Coast newspapers, with headlines suggesting that we were about to see a rerun of the 1930s.

This time, the impact was not quite so cataclysmic. Nonetheless, I was slightly amazed by the exaggerated response, both on television and on the news wires, to some remarks I made in interviews concerning the less-than-brilliant record of much of the Wall Street establishment. The interviews were in connection with a new book of mine, and I merely reiterated the sentiment that I had conveyed to you earlier in our newsletters: that the wild selling by institutional investors this past fall had proved only that "they are world champions at panicking and hysterical overreactions." You would think, from some of the ensuing accounts, that the Pope had questioned Catholicism!

Yet, as it turns out, my expressions of moderate disdain for the conventional wisdom of most of Wall Street are beginning to look distinctly understated. First, because the sensible individual investors who declined to join the stampede are already looking much brighter than the lofty institutional gents who rushed to don their lemming—or is that "lemon"?—costumes. Second, because we have seen, in recent weeks, an even greater outbreak of mass fallibility on the part of some of the highest-paid securities analysts in the business.

Don't misunderstand me: anybody can be wrong, and sensible people respond to new information. But what has happened lately to any number of stocks is that earnings "disappointments" appear to have totally shocked the analysts who were supposed to be clued in to these companies, after which the stocks were immediately sold off brutally, right at the opening bell. And many analysts who had loved these stocks a day earlier promptly lowered their recommendations—presumably on the assumption that some idiot out there might be tempted to buy low.

This faulty behavior demonstrates three significant flaws in much of the analytical community. First, as many an individual investor has noted with disgust, it's excruciatingly hard to get a "sell" recommendation out of these cats. While the investment business is famously profane,

that's the one word most of them can't quite bring themselves to utter. The inability to get their usually hyperac-
tive mouths around the word "sell" is not, I suspect, an
indication of the sensitivity of their souls. Investment
bankers make more money by issuing securities for companies than they do by providing customers with unhedged
analysis, and despite all the talk of a "Chinese wall"
between those two functions, I must confess a certain occasional skepticism about the total frankness of the operation.

Second, analysts like to be liked. It's a perfectly human
instinct, but securities analysts are like foreign correspondents: as I found while in that earlier incarnation, foreign
correspondents are often most useful when they are least
liked by the governments of the countries they are cover-
ing. Telling it like it is is rarely a passport to popularity.

Third, many analysts don't want to be out there with a
"buy" recommendation on a stock that has just taken a
spectacular tumble. Not only is this often a source of derision (and possibly limited career opportunity) within their
own firms, but it is likely to run contrary to the actions of
their biggest clients. As we saw again this past month,
when the end of a year is approaching, money managers
typically scurry to divest themselves of anything that will
not look pretty in their published year-end portfolios.
Hence, for example, the continuing market troubles of
many solid technology companies that, I'm convinced, will
begin to look more attractive again as 1998 unfolds.

So while I was a tad surprised at the apparent newsworthiness of my comment that many a Wall Street tycoon would make an excellent short sale—selling him at his own estimate of himself and then buying him back for what he was really worth—I think, in retrospect, that I may have been too gentle. Having spent my entire life in journalism, but in recent decades finding myself increasingly being interviewed by journalists, I have an unusual dual perspective on the ever-controversial subject of the media. What I tell business leaders and others is that the same thing is true of journalism that is true of a number of other professions, notably including Wall Street: outsiders tend habitually to overrate the malice, and underrate the incompetence.

From "Who Loves Ya? Tender Words for Wall Street and Beyond"
—February 1998

A few Valentines for the deserving, and otherwise:

To all our newly lovelorn friends in Asia—

Thought you might need a little special cheering up this February. You have just found out, to the kind of distress that knows no continent, that financial affection is even more fickle than the more-carnal kind.

Shucks, just a few months ago, legions of wide-eyed Wall Street analysts were hastening to your exotic boudoirs to court you with terms of boundless endearment. Not only was the 21st Century sure to be Asia's, they proclaimed, but maybe you'd wind up with the 20th, too. Now, these former suitors are hooting with callous contempt, contending that all your emperors are really just naked, and not too pretty a sight, at that. A little currency crisis here, a few tales of corruption there, and your once-supercharged markets are cut off at the knees, as hordes of inconstant Western analysts desert you and race to book the bridal suites in Paris and Berlin.

But be of stout heart, Asian sweethearts. There's a lesson in this that might be worth learning in such other capitals as Moscow and (dare I say it?) Washington, as well: the trappings of capitalism are fine, but they work best in an atmosphere of maximum freedom. When governments step in to "help" their people, favoritism and regulatory hindrances are seldom far behind. And in the end, they can bring unhappy surprises to even the most promising economies.

Don't make the mistake of petulantly blaming your troubles on Western imperialists, money-center banks or George Soros: look to your strengths, which have flourished dramatically as freedom has expanded, and tend that garden well. You'll be back, sooner than many people think, and smart investors will be waiting to greet you with a hug.

To a corporate CEO merrily leaping from one company to another, gathering rosebuds while he may—

I know this is going to come as a terrible shock to you, especially if you've been hiding behind your public-relations department, but not everybody out there loves you. Really! A lot of folks get downright piqued when you land in a new company town, fire everybody in sight, sell any division not growing at least 20% a year, cash in your options, collect a massive exit bonus and skip town on the redeye. People are funny that way.

So, what's a well-trained MBA to do? Don't let them get you down. Wall Street still loves you, your golf game is definitely improving, and how important actually is it to have friends in your old age? And if you ever feel the need of warm and affectionate reinforcement from a truly constant admirer, heck, just look in the mirror.

To everybody who's worrying about this month's credit-card bills—

If it's any consolation, my darling, you're not alone in your moment of anguish. Tens of millions of other Americans are wondering why this "perfect" economy they keep reading about has somehow neglected to visit *their* neighborhood. In the more than a decade that we have been polling for our annual TV special, *Louis Rukeyser's Money Guide*, 1998 was the first time when more people said the country seemed to be doing better than they were. So what's a poor, patriotic, upward-striving American to do? You got it: go deeper into debt. By late 1997, consumers had accumulated a whopping $525 billion in credit-card debt, with a record 5.25% going unpaid. After all, most people think saving and investing is no fun; folks want instant gratification, and they would prefer to have it yesterday.

So, what message can those of us who try to build wealth send to those who just want to build a bigger tab? Check out the color of a Valentine heart: if it just warms your soul, enjoy—but if it matches the permanent color of your bank account, it may be time to kiss a few indulgences goodbye. Don't worry: you don't have to tell the neighbors, and your secret is safe with me.

To the chairman of the Federal Reserve Board—

Nobody has to tell you about the power of romance, Alan Greenspan—not after a year in which you distinguished yourself by marrying delightfully and doing virtually nothing whatsoever to the American economy. And we appreciate it.

Roses are red, violets are blue, we like it when the Fed knows there's nothing to do.

P.S. If you get totally bored, a little rate cut or two wouldn't go amiss. Meanwhile: kiss, kiss.

To the bond ghouls—

Just wanted you to know how emotionally moved, and grateful, we are that you have given us another successful year of trading against you. In 1994, in 1996 and again in 1997, each time you stampeded in the absurd belief that a whiff of prosperity inevitably leads to a bad dose of inflation, we've been waiting to scoop up what you were discarding.

So, dear ghouls, don't change a hair for us, not if you care for us. We'll be waiting eagerly for you to give us another chance to buy low and sell high. And we love you for it.

And, as always, a special, oversized, satin-and-lace Valentine to the folks we truly couldn't live without: the stock market's perennial bears—

Oh, I know some of you are feeling a mite testy these days. Not only does the market keep going up, year after year, despite your learned warnings that it has been dangerously overpriced since roughly 1932. Not only do your occasional short and happy interludes of terror, from 1987 to 1997, somehow never lead to anything like the enduring disaster for which you yearn. But, most awful of all, in the lonely dark of night, you sometimes begin to suspect, yourself, that you're not just a heck of a lot poorer than you might have been, but even (just possibly, is it conceivable, could it ever be true) maybe even terribly wrong.

Take heart, my gloomy friend. You're sure to have company again every time the great bull market momentarily falters, as it surely will continue to do from time to time.

When Asia trembles, some Wall Streeters will instantly sell any company whose executives are thought to have visited a Thai restaurant. When any commodity from myrrh to ginger encounters above-average demand, your counterparts in the bond market will panic about inflation, and there may be a passing fright in the equities market, led by institutional investors and other slow-witted types. When the economy's pace slows a bit, as it is likely to do in the next few months, you can count on some fools prematurely howling: "Deflationary depression!"

Meanwhile, those of us of a more-cheerful bent will remain preoccupied with such trivial consolations as a powerfully competitive American economy and a world that, despite the well-publicized bumps, is actually getting to be a better place to live and do business. Leave us to our naïveté and our profits. We love you, honey, and we couldn't do it without you.

From "Marching On Like a Lion, This Bull's Not on the Lam"
—March 1998

I have advised you all along that one of the best things
going for the long-term bull market was its tendency to get
awfully worried awfully fast. And, as we have seen repeatedly in recent months, this is a market that severely, if not
unduly, punishes any company whose earnings fail to measure up to the estimates of the ever-haughty, though rarely-
omniscient, analysts. This self-correcting mechanism, while
painful to those whose holdings get battered, is highly useful in dehydrating market froth and solidifying the basis for
future advances. But the other side of the equation is significant, too—and the simple truth is that most 1998 earnings
reports have been coming in ahead of estimates. This indi-
cates that the powerful restructuring of U.S. industry, now
indisputably the most-competitive on the globe, is far from
played out as a market propellant. As for Asia, while its full
impact has not yet been felt over here, there is increasing
support for the notion that the tradeoff between weaker consumer economies and cheaper exports will ultimately prove
positive for many American companies.

Finally, just as an army marches on its stomach (an
insight of the renowned Corsican speculator, Napoleon
Bonaparte), so the fuel of finance is cash. And it keeps
coming in. The convoluted changes in the IRA rules will
be of some help there, though less than if they had been
less restrictive and "targeted." More important is that the

average American increasingly sees stocks as a sensible place to be: inflows into stock mutual funds set another record in 1997 ($231 billion), and when stocks started to move again in late January, so did the inflows. Less noticed has been the supercharged effect of corporate merger activity, which generated $920 billion last year, including $500 billion in cash. Add to that the continuing trend toward corporate buybacks of stock (rather than high dividends, which would be taxable at shareholders' most-lofty rates), and you see a money machine that is scarcely about to grind to a halt.

So watch the short-term "technicals," if you will, but don't get talked out of sticking with the bull. He's a long way from being ready for permanent pasture.

From "Three Coulds Aside, This Market Still Can"
—April 1998

I realize that I am violating official protocol even by
mentioning the word "recession." (When economist
Alfred Kahn was serving in the Carter Administration,
he was so chastised for daring to discuss the possibility
publicly that he subsequently used the euphemism
"banana" every time he meant "recession.") But the
reality is that the sequence that leads to most bear markets is not at all mysterious. Bear markets are an attempt
(not always accurate) to forecast a recession. And what
triggers the forecast is often either purely economic,
such as growth-killing interest-rate hikes, or purely
financial, such as the kind of euphoria that dissolves the
famous wall of worry.

Neither extreme is yet on the horizon, in my judgment,
though clearly things are not as explosively bullish, at
these lofty levels, as they were a few months ago, when I
was much more lonely in my optimism. A correction could
certainly come at any time—such midcourse corrections
are actually healthy for an ongoing bull market—but,
based on what we know now, I'm convinced that the really
big bad bear is still going to have to hibernate for quite a
while longer.

So, weed out your mistakes, sure (everybody makes
them), but continue to buy selectively and don't be
frightened when the market shows, as it inevitably will

from time to time, that even this prodigious bull occasionally has to inhale as well as exhale. By any reasonable long-term perspective, my friend, you ain't seen nothin' yet.

From "Trust the Best Advice in Wall Street: Ours And Yours" —April 1998

Gosh, who can you trust these days? The President of the United States plays "he said, she said" with an ever-burgeoning collection of disenchanted ladies. Assorted United Nations officials assure us, with perfectly straight faces, that Saddam Hussein is actually one of the sweetest guys you'd ever hope to meet. And the Beardstown Ladies turn out to be, in reality, (gasp) below-average investors.

It looks as if April Fool's Day came early this year.

And the Man of the Year is likely to be P.T. Barnum.

So what's a poor mutual-fund shareholder to do? Happily, you've known for some time that you can't trust the conventional wisdom of the routine financial-advice community, which found out years ago that the easiest way to get your attention was to shout "Fire!" in a crowded market at least seven or eight times annually.

You've long since learned that when a stockbroker suggests that you sell A and buy B, he may have more than your long-term welfare in mind. (Doctors, it has been said, bury their mistakes. Brokers just take a second commission. And then sometimes a third—if you can be convinced to buy something else.) In the short run, at least, you might get the impression that this is a business where nothing succeeds like failure.

And, finally, you know now to view with profound skepticism the next set of highly touted newcomers to the scene—from the dear, hapless Beardstown Ladies to the smart-alecky online adolescents—who periodically con innocent media types into believing that something marvelously insightful has just been discovered, that nobody ever thought of before. You betcha.

What you can trust, I hope, is (1) us—a trust we never take for granted, but strive to earn anew with every issue of our newsletters—and (2) that stunning face you see in the mirror every morning. Successful investing is not rocket science, however many new computer programs come drifting through cyberspace. It starts with knowing yourself, including your genuine needs and your true ability to handle risk. The market is a habitually frenetic worrywart, and its violent mood changes can be fatally unsettling if you don't prepare yourself for them in advance.

Having failed to find omniscience in any other adviser, we are never so foolish as to claim it for ourselves. Speaking for myself, over the decades I've probably made every dumb mistake it's possible to make in investing. But I've tried to learn from them, and my batting average gets better all the time. Nothing would make me happier than to help improve yours, too.

One of the most important lessons, which applies to all of us, is not to treat the market like a casino. If you do, you will encounter casino odds—and remember, it's not the customers who own those fancy buildings. Sure, it's fun to try to guess exactly which way the market is going to jump next. But nobody—repeat, nobody—does it flawlessly, and you should never bet the ranch on such a "feeling in my bones." Far better to accumulate solid funds and stocks, and then hold them with a long-term perspective, while periodically monitoring your portfolio to eliminate the inevitable disappointments (with funds, primarily those that fail, for a sustained period, to match others with the same style of investment) and replace them with authentically superior choices. We can help you there, and try to each month, but the person you have to rely on in the end is no one but you.

Not even the Beardstown Ladies.

From "Staying Rooted in the Market Can Help Your Portfolio Bloom"
—May 1998

As that eminent financial authority Gertrude Stein so aptly put it, "Rose is a rose is a rose." Call me crazy, but I always thought Gert hit the nail on the head with that one (or at least the flower on the petal). Despite a lifetime of floral observation, I've never found any evidence that a rose is, say, a chrysanthemum or even a jack-in-the-pulpit—though, to be perfectly honest, I haven't checked every one of the religious channels currently available. The stock market seems to agree with Ms. Stein, too, though it has given her famous line a slightly different spin: it rose and it rose and it rose.

With the Dow up more than 50% in just eighteen months, defying all the gloomsters who kept telling us to get out of the garden (and mowing down thousand-point marks as if they were dandelions), it seems appropriate to hand out a few May flowers of our own on the investment scene.

An elegant orchid goes to Laszlo Birinyi, who makes it all sound so easy: all you have to do is follow every single stock trade, and then the market itself will tell you exactly where it's heading. Got that? Then stop all your nail-biting, and get to work. It shouldn't take more than 10 years to get your own computer programmed properly, and what else do you have going in the next decade that's more important? Or, perhaps, you might just prefer to let

86

Laszlo and his formidable data banks (the best of which, I'm convinced, is inside his head) attend to the grubby details for you, and continue to report regularly in my newsletters and television program. Enjoy.

Stinkweeds, on the other hand, go to all those "prudent" folks who are perennially trying to scare us off. Even some of the loftiest Establishment entities in Wall Street have begun to wake up to the foolishness of not recognizing that *every* time is different. Take Salomon Smith Barney, which in January flinched and unwisely lowered its recommended equity allocation from 55% to 50%, just before the market made its latest marvelous move upward. (Clearly, somebody there hadn't been reading his *Louis Rukeyser's Wall Street*. For shame!) Brokerage firms rarely apologize, as you may have noticed, but this one at least had the sense to name a new allocator, John Manley, who reversed the previous recommendation and raised the suggested equity portion all the way to 65%. His reasons are worth noting for anyone who still believes the old tune that the stock market has to crash because it is "overvalued."

Noting that both valuation and earnings momentum have been notoriously poor timing devices over the years, Manley zeroed in on one of the gloomsters' favorite facts: that the market's price-to-sales ratio has doubled in the past four years. The last time that happened, he noted wryly, was 1954 to 1958. And the market did indeed go on to reach a peak in that cycle—but not till *eight years* later! (Gosh, let's all rush to sell everything before sundown tomorrow.) Manley is considerably more impressed by the drop in long-term interest rates over the past 12 months, which he regards as a more-reliable precursor of a still-healthy stock market. Give that man a posy.

As for Salomon Smith Barney's parent company, Travelers Group, its dynamic CEO Sanford Weill is clearly entitled to our finest Venus's-flytrap. Sandy is the most voracious acquirer in the financial world, his latest and greatest trophy being the $85-billion megamerger with Citicorp, which not only sent both stocks soaring but has already led to a historic round of marriages and serious dating throughout the banking and financial-services industries. The Citicorp surprise was so beautifully engineered that it looked like an absolutely perfect deal in every respect but one, which is that some people thought it happened to be illegal. But that minor detail (a relic of the outmoded 1933 Glass-Steagall Act, whose repeal is long overdue) didn't seem to be spoiling anybody's party in the first weeks after the announcement. Indeed, if this blockbuster consolidation spurs a wider look at the entire panoply of U.S. antitrust legislation, much of it a century out of date amid the internationally competitive realities facing America today, Sandy will deserve even more bouquets.

Then there ought to be room in this floral arrangement for a few mums and glads. The mums, I would hope—though vainly, I fear—should be those who, year after year, besiege us with alarms about this being "as good as it gets," and urging us, if not to flee in panic, at least to "take a little off the table." (By now, if you've been following the advice of many of them, the only thing left on your table will be a bent fork.) "I'm sorry, I blew it," may be too much for us to expect them to say, but it would be nice if they could at least consider a few months of staying absolutely mum. Gee, guys, don't you think we've earned it?

The glads, on the other hand, are those who have suffered (and in many cases are still suffering) through the woes of some of our largest technology companies. As I write this, the subject is still highly controversial, with learned analysts coming out with diametrically opposed views on such ailing behemoths as Intel and Compaq. The reason to be glad is that the latest news from these companies is no worse than expected, and in some respects better. My own view is unhedged: this is a tough period, with computer prices plunging and product cycles accelerating, and there will be more difficult months ahead, but anyone with a reasonable time frame, looking ahead a couple of years, should regard this as a chance to buy and plant some beauties for the early 21st Century. Get your hardy perennials when they're cheap.

From "Growth or Value? Keeping Your Cool is Always in Style"
—August 1998

One of the most entertaining, and enlightening, confrontations at our Louis Rukeyser Investment Conferences in recent years has been that between Foster Friess and Mario Gabelli. I deliberately put them on the same panel, because Foster, the lead manager of the Brandywine Fund, has been an outstandingly articulate advocate of "growth" investing, while Mario, chairman of Gabelli Funds, is a similarly effective spokesman for the "value" camp.

Last year, for example, when Mario dramatized his then-current recommendation of American Express by holding up his green credit card, Foster got a roar out of the crowd of 10,000 by saying that if Mario had been a growth-stock investor, he would have had a gold card by now. Gabelli was unfazed: "That's a perfect example of the problem with 'growth' investors," he said. "A 'value' investor knows that the green American Express card is the better bargain."

Who's right about the best approach to investing? The only true answer is that they both are. Over the years, stocks will respond to their companies' increases in earnings, as the "growth" investors contend—and no sensible "value" investor can afford to be indifferent to that trend. And no sensible "growth" investor should want heedlessly to overpay for a stock, a rash act that can make the unwary investor susceptible to some of the market's most jolting downturns. At different periods, the market will

favor one style of investing over another. The most successful long-term managers stick to a consistent style. But
they don't ignore the rest of the equation, either: nothing
is nicer than buying what the market thinks of as a
"value" stock and selling it long after the market has perceived it as a "growth" stock. Bargains are sometimes in
the eye of the beholder; profits, on the other hand, cross
party lines.

Recent months, as it happens, have seen a remarkable triumph for Mario, and an acknowledged defeat for
Foster, on a subject on which both the opposing camps
should have long since agreed: the folly of trying to time
the markets. And there's a lesson there for all us humble
mutual-fund shareholders as well.

After the brief U.S. market meltdown that followed the
Asian collapse late last year, Foster concluded that a
crash was imminent and that he had better run for the
hills. That kind of emotion is perfectly natural for any
investor when the headlines are screaming "Crisis!"—but
the best thing to do when that panic strikes is usually to
take two aspirins (and don't call your broker in the morning). Instead, Foster sold stocks as if they were toxic. His
$8-billion fund went to 78% cash. (I am not making these
numbers up.) And he stayed in that unfortunate position
when, in the cool light of morning, the markets made a
quick recovery and began another historic rally.

Now Foster, in addition to being a very nice man, is a
very honest one. And instead of providing alibis for this
neophyte-style mistake, he has now fully and undefensive-

ly admitted his error. "We were wrong," he says, "and I take the blame for that." Brandywine's cash position today is in the low single digits. (Says a rueful Foster, "If you're not humble in the investment business, it only means you haven't been in it long enough.")

My point is not to beat up on my friend, who has so graciously acknowledged his aberration, but to highlight how tempting it is to overreact to short-term market developments. Such activities may be particularly unfortunate for mutual-fund managers, since most shareholders are paying them to fulfill their promised function (in Brandywine's case, to buy growth stocks) and not to attempt the kind of asset allocation that individuals can do for themselves. The truth is, as I have so often tried to point out in this space, that nobody in this world can correctly call short-term market movements with any consistency. You wouldn't always know this, if you read the awful hype in so many financial magazines and newsletters, but it happens to be absolutely true. Year after year, much more money is lost than made by those trying futilely to stay one jump ahead of the market's passing neuroses.

Which takes me to Mario's triumph. This self-described "stuck-in-the-wool, Graham & Dodd type"—an old-fashioned "value" investor—had the year of his life in 1997, a period when most prominent investors of similar bent were conspicuously missing large chunks of the market's lavish profits, on the self-righteous grounds that it had become far too pricey to merit their august involvement.

It wasn't that Mario had no concerns about the market's valuation; he did, and does. He knows that no market ever goes straight up, and he worries about certain historical benchmarks. But he figures, as it were, that that's not what he's being paid to do. He's being paid to discern meaningful business trends and to find individual stocks that meet his standards. And that he has continued, resolutely, to do. Far more important (and far more successful) than his overall market judgments has been his ability to find stocks that most investors were neglecting. As he put it to me the other day, "It really was not what we bought in 1997 but what we bought in 1995 and 1996: domestic businesses that were somewhat out of favor."

No market timer could have told Mario precisely when the market would vindicate these judgments. He clearly didn't know the answer to that himself. But he held to what he did know, and was notably patient. That's something we all can emulate. In my view, there is no one single way to make the most money in Wall Street—there is merit, over time, in both the "growth" and "value" camps, and intelligently diversified mutual-fund investors will keep a foot in both— but there is one pretty certain way to lose money: panicking in the face of temporary adversity. Fear is the most powerful emotion in finance, which is why conscienceless marketers of financial trash try perennially to exploit it. When even as brilliant and experienced an investor as Foster Friess can be swept away by it, it's a clear message for the rest of us to remember the next time the market goes south and the end of the world seems nigh. ■

LOUIS RUKEYSER

on

THE ECONOMY, GOVERNMENT & POLITICS

PART TWO

Louis Rukeyser

on

The Economy, Government & Politics

From "Alan's Show of Courage—The First Hit of the New Fall Season"
—October 1996

If the 1996 election were a sitcom, it would have been canceled long ago. The characters aren't plausible, the dialogue is dreadful, the acting is transparent and the plot is totally incoherent. The best thing about it is that it faces certain termination November 5, after which it will again be permissible for rational human beings to talk some sense about the American economy.

Happily for investors, one fellow who seems to have resisted the political rhetoric is my old friend Alan Greenspan, who has been my guest on television no fewer than seven times, and who was capable of thinking quite reasonably—and even speaking quite lucidly—before he returned to the intellectual snake pit inside the Beltway. The conventional view is that the Greenspan-led Federal Reserve was simply being chicken by standing pat on interest rates at its much-ballyhooed September 24 meeting, but my own conclusion is the opposite. Rather than bowing to pressures to avoid roiling the waters just before an election, Greenspan was actually hanging tough against manifold extraneous pressures. The result should be good for the economy, and good for investors.

Don't expect every segment of the investment community to recognize this all at once. The bond ghouls have made a profession in this decade of giving new meaning to the phrase "can't stand prosperity." Give them even a moderate pickup from the stagnant 1995 economy, and they are crying not just wolf but an entire pack of the ravenous beasts. The ultra-jittery traders have continued to operate for much of 1996 under the fascinating, if wholly incorrect, philosophy that a better economy means worse inflation. Never mind that our economic history is chockfull of examples of vigorous growth with moderating inflation (and, for that matter, of declining growth with rising inflation). Somebody told them that it was sophisticated to run for the hills every time somebody else landed a job, and their knees still jerk rapidly in that direction. But not, I suspect, forever.

As the true master of monetary policy, Nobel laureate Milton Friedman, has just pointed out again, the sole achievable task in that area is not to rein in national prosperity—or to set arbitrary limits on how fast an economy should be allowed to grow—but to focus on producing a rate of money growth moderate enough to keep inflation under control. And that the Fed has clearly done. Astonishingly, especially for anyone who has been foolish enough to succumb to the rhetoric of the interest-rate gloomsters in the 1990s, inflation is as close to nonexistent as we have seen in more than a generation. The critically important "core" rates of both producer and consumer inflation, which get the Fed's closest continuing attention, were both within a tenth of a percent of no change at all in the most recent reports. So ignore the chatter about the alleged obligation of the Fed to "take away the punch bowl just when the party is getting good"; the authentic danger is that monetary chefs reading from an outmoded recipe book will prematurely poison the punch—and thus the U.S. economy.

Score one for Alan Greenspan. He plainly resisted heavy pressure from within the Fed, especially from those who leaked a report that regional Fed governors favored an interest-rate increase. And he stood tough in the face of unsolicited advice from the International Monetary Fund, whose unfailing prescriptions for prosperity-through-austerity have torpedoed more third-world economies than drought and pestilence combined.

I'm as concerned about true inflation as anyone in the Chicago bond pits; in fact, way back in 1969, when the problem was light years away from the standard American consciousness, I wrote and hosted on ABC-TV the first national hour on the subject (the title was nearly as long as the program: "The Great Dollar Robber: Can We Arrest Inflation?"), but I have never seen much value in diligently fighting the last economic war. The task now is to get the American economy moving significantly more robustly from here to the Twenty-first Century, and the Fed's September forbearance is a sign to investors and average citizens alike that monetary policy will not sabotage that effort.

From "Food For Thought: A Six-Course Meal to Fatten Your Wallet"
—November 1996

Six reasons for investors to be grateful at Thanksgiving 1996:

(1) The country is a heck of a lot stronger than its politicians.

Americans who have suffered through one of the most intellectually vacuous Presidential campaigns since the invention of the ballot box may understandably be a mite concerned about the future. My advice is to relax and enjoy your turkey. Happily, these wet-finger-in-the-wind "leaders" are far less crucial to our economy's prospects than they so grandly pretend. If I had to make my financial forecasts based on the economic brainpower of our politicians—in either party—I'd be the biggest bear who ever growled. But while they can and do slow us down, they can't quite stop us in our tracks. So ignore the claims that one side's crowing brings the dawn, while the other side's cackling produces the night. The real news, and the real future, will be found in the impressive competitive condition of private American industry, a streamlining and revitalization that has become increasingly evident over the past 15 years. Which leads us to Reason #2...

(2) U.S. productivity is on a roll.
Real wages in the U.S. finally show signs of being

able to shake out of the doldrums in which they have
languished for the past 20 years. And while the constitutionally jittery bond ghouls incorrectly view this as a
sure sign of resurgent inflation, the reality is that
improvements in U.S. productivity make it possible at
last for workers to live better without reigniting the
inflationary fires. World competitive pressures act as a
discipline against some of the routine excesses of the
past, both in union halls and in sloppy management.
Barely a decade ago, the doomsters invaded the best-
seller lists with tomes declaring that the U.S. was on an
inevitable downhill slide as compared with our overseas
rivals. Some of our more vocal political figures still
haven't gotten the word (so what else is new?), but the
U.S. is again unmistakably the world's industrial titan,
setting the global pace in business after business. Tales
of alleged American inferiority would be greeted by hol-
low laughter today in Europe and Japan. And one reason for *that* is...

*(3) Our government hasn't yet been able to "help" us as
much as it would have liked to.*
Roaming the world as a foreign correspondent for more
than a decade, I was able to observe how a variety of vastly
different nations organized themselves economically. The
inescapable conclusion was that no politician anywhere on
the planet had ever actually created a rupee's worth of prosperity. Politicians are pretty good at "redistributing" wealth
that somebody else has created, and they can be wondrous-

ly effective at destroying wealth, but its creation depends on invention, scientific progress and, most of all, human toil. The reason this is not more generally recognized is not difficult to discern. Envy is one of the strongest emotions, and vote-seeking politicians routinely play to it with abandon. But the good news is how little they have actually implemented in recent years, as compared with the supposedly more compassionate European societies, where the governments' extensive "social nets" are intended to protect their people from the slings and arrows of outrageous marketplaces. These "social nets," it turns out, have done everything except what they were supposed to do. With all the talk about brutal U.S. "downsizing" and assorted other allegedly heartless labor policies, the U.S. in recent years has produced not just the strongest economy in the industrial world but the lowest unemployment. It's probably beyond the capacity of our politicians on either side ever to acknowledge this, but in reality their frustrating "gridlock" has been our own green light. This even applies to...

(4) The budget deficit has been shrinking—for reasons the political debate would rather we didn't understand.

No, it's certainly not because of the latest succession of tax increases—which have simply served, as ever, to retard growth and encourage bureaucrats to dream up new spending schemes. There are three fundamental causes for the lower deficits, and neither Bill Clinton nor Newt Gingrich has much to do with any of them. First, the U.S. won the cold war. I know it's been a long time ago, as compared with the average American memory span, but it really did happen, I assure you, and it was a pretty significant event. In budget terms, it has meant a significant decline in defense spending—a decline that would have occurred, inevitably, even if Norman Schwarzkopf had been elected President in 1992. Second, the economy is neither as bad as Clinton said in 1992 nor as Bob Dole said in 1996; the longest U.S. peacetime expansion was briefly interrupted by Saddam Hussein in 1990, but the economy has been moving forward again for nearly six years. This has paid off both in higher revenues and in lower social expenditures. Third, public consciousness of, and concern about, deficits has intensified to the point where even the most profligate politicians have to pay attention, which limits the tradition- al grandiosity of their proposals. None of this means that we can forget about federal spending; the real booby trap lies ahead, in the unchecked entitlement programs, but the only certainty now is that, however imperfectly, we're going to have to begin to come to grips with that one, too—even though no campaigning politician is likely to talk honestly about it. There's hope even here, though, because...

(5) People are not as terminally stupid as campaigning politicians seem to believe.

For all the glib assurances from both sides that the fur- thest thing from their minds is to make any meaningful changes in such ultra-sacred cows as Social Security, lit- tle voters are not as easy to fool as they used to be. And this turns out to be something to be grateful for, too, because Americans are acting on their skepticism in a highly positive way. One major example is the greatly increased concern with private retirement planning. Baby Boomers, and Generation Xers as well, recognize that while the system can and should keep its promises to the elderly, the day of reckoning for younger Americans cannot be indefinitely postponed. The huge new inflows of savings into private investments, dramatically but by no means exclusively mutual funds, not only show a degree of common sense that bodes well for the nation's future— but are an enduringly positive sign for the long-term future of the financial markets. And there, to our delight, we find...

(6) Bearishness remains wonderfully high.

Perhaps the most amazing thing about this entire extraordinary period is that, even as thousand-point marks on the Dow have tumbled with brisk abandon, the underlying mood in the financial markets has remained remarkably subdued. We've seen this in any number of technical statistics, but possibly the most telling evidence has been the way the hysterical pessimists resurface with every passing selloff. Let the market briefly plummet, as it did in July, and you're immediately subjected to still-another round of terrifying "sell all stocks" signals—which often are exposed as nutty even before their frenzied mailings can reach potential subscribers. Let's hope these turkeys never cease their clucking. Meanwhile, keep the faith and have a happy, peaceful—and grateful—Thanksgiving.

From "Let the Economy Grow? What a Capital Idea!"
—June 1997

Another kind of pause seems to be in the works in
Washington: a pause in the mindless overtaxation of capital
that otherwise would surely come back to haunt us when
the vibrant private economy falters. Ideologues have dominated the tax debate through the 1990s, and the strength of
the economy has allowed them to get away with it. The historic restructuring of U.S. industry over the past 15 years
throws off so many benefits that we have even been able to
survive our politicians. Regrettably, there is still no sign of
enlightened action on either side of the aisle to reduce the
punitive, soak-the-successful tax-rate increases under the
past two presidents. But something resembling at least a
mild reality check seems to be occurring in the realm of
capital gains.

You'd never guess it from what passes for most media
comments on this subject, which generally cast it as a
rich-vs.-poor issue, but there is no issue more central to
future economic growth and rising living standards for all
Americans than the excessive taxation of savings and
investment in this country. Alan Greenspan, when he was
still in private life and thus able to speak the truth without
glancing nervously at the polls or the politicians, told me
flatly that he was convinced that the only appropriate tax
rate for capital gains was "zero." This is the cutting edge
of the creation of better jobs in America, he observed, and

those who fret that the government might be sacrificing some revenue don't realize how very much more it would then be collecting further down the income stream.

Indeed, perhaps the most remarkable thing about cutting the capital-gains tax is that it pays off in ways that many other tax reductions—however desirable in and of themselves—do not. First, the government collects a lot more revenue from lower rates, as investors sitting on long-held gains decide to cash in. (The capital-gains tax is uniquely voluntary: if you don't sell, you don't pay it.) Second, as sellers reinvest, presumably in more newly desirable areas, this fuels economic expansion and higher government revenues. Those doubting this, or buffaloed by the so-called static analysis of the Washington budget "experts" (who view any dollar of tax cuts as a dollar lost to the government), need only review the history of previous capital-gains-tax reductions, notably the recent ones in 1978 and 1981: without fail, they "surprised" all the conventional forecasters by feeding back huge new revenues over the years. I suspect it will happen again.

From "Three 'Coulds' Aside, This Market Still Can"
—April 1998

Overkill by the Fed is the most usual reason for bull markets to end. Traditionally, the nation's monetary authorities seemed to know only two ways to drive America's money car: with their foot all the way down on the accelerator or all the way down on the brake. This jerky go-stop pattern was perhaps the most significant factor in creating the boom-bust cycle that became so depressingly familiar in this century.

But people do learn sometimes, even in Washington, and Alan Greenspan is an awesomely detailed student of history. He should not be overpraised in this department, despite the media tendency to venerate almost any sitting Fed chairman as irreplaceable. His Fed was guilty of serious overtightening as recently as 1994 and 1995, and (lest we forget) this helped produce a financial-market meltdown and the weakest nonrecession year for the economy since World War II. I'm not sure he's ready to deliver a *mea culpa* yet, but the man has an admirable tendency to watch and learn—and his refusal to bend to the habitual inflation hawks since then has been correct and commendable. The economy, and the investment markets, have benefited mightily.

From "How an Investing Revolution Is Changing Your Future"
May 1998

There is no more dramatic evidence of the change in the American psyche over the past generation than the cryptic name "401(k)." Until the mid-1980s, most Americans wouldn't have known what you were talking about; they might have assumed, if you murmured "401(k)," that you were either a code-speaking secret agent for the Evil Empire or an aging ex-quarterback harking back to his days as a play-caller. Not today; indeed, I suspect that more Americans know what "401(k)" means than can tell you the name of the Chief Justice of the Supreme Court. And it was reported in April that the assets of 401(k) retirement plans have now surpassed $1 trillion.

America—and American investment—will never be the same. Until this past generation, it was relatively easy for the average citizen to assume that big institutions were safely in command of his or her life. Big government would provide Social Security, and big businesses and/or big unions could be counted on to supplement it with a reliable pension system. You betcha.

One by one, the great institutions revealed their clay feet. And, characteristically, it was too much government, rather than too little, that doomed the traditional private-pension programs. As regulations to "protect" us from evil employers mushroomed, more and more companies simply ended their increasingly burdensome plans. And with Social Security taxes already soaring, to support an ominously rickety institution for the 21st Century, there was no chance that Mama Government would pack the extra-calorie lunch the corporations were canceling.

To the rescue came the newly authorized 401(k) plans, which differed in one tremendously significant respect from what they replaced: now the employees, not the employers, were given control of their investment choices. It was a forced course in financial education for millions of working Americans, and they have passed it in a way that will inevitably reshape the broader political-social agenda as well.

When I was a boy, the prevailing culture spoke of "guarantees," usually from government. Not just bare-bones support programs like Social Security were to be "guaranteed" in the brave new world. Workers were to get "a guaranteed annual wage"—I kid you not; it was a major negotiating point there for a while. And, at the end of a lifetime of guaranteed wages and guaranteed employment, we would all be guaranteed a lovely pension, invested as directed by the geniuses who signed our paychecks. Guaranteed.

We are wiser today. Ever-increasing numbers of Americans have discovered that those putative Wizards of Oz were really no more magical than you or me. And so the new investor class has grown, learning along the way that its members have now become the capitalists that many of them once denounced, as youthful ideologues, and that it's not all bad. Karl Marx wanted the workers to own the means of production, and so they do today—though in a way that turns Marxism on its loony head.

Mutual funds were made to order for the 401(k) Revolution. Some 270,000 companies now offer 401(k)s to more than 25 million American workers, and the share those self-directed employees have been putting in mutual funds has shown fantastic growth: more than doubling, to 37%, just since 1990. A wonderfully rising stock market has helped, of course, but so has the recognition that long-term financial planning requires taking the kind of sensible risks that government "guarantors" were once trying to protect us from.

It's fashionable to be quite doomy about some of these developments, and to argue that vulnerable little workers will be devastated the next time we have a bear market. I don't buy it. First, the percentage in funds is still on the low side of what would be right for most people. Second, as employees continue to work and take a long-term view of the money they are investing in the plans each year, they are in fact showing a more-rational investment approach than the giant in-and-outers who scorn (and usually underperform) the public.

Further evidence abounds. March 1998 was the record month for net inflows into mutual funds—401(k)s or otherwise: $37.5 billion, of which $27.5 billion went into stock funds. Again, the resilient market helped mightily. But so did other factors, including the lure of the new Roth IRAs, which tax contributions but allow the money to grow and be withdrawn tax-free upon retirement. Combined with the ever

more evident good sense of the average investor—still counterintuitive to many old-fashioned analysts—this is additional powerful ammunition for a long-term, self-reliant
approach.

The only problem with 401(k)s is that they often unduly
limit the employees' investment choices. To that extent,
self-directed IRAs have the edge, as of course do other
forms of direct investment. I would hope that as the tens of
millions of new investors gain more experience and confidence, they will apply pressure to remove such restrictions
on their free choice. There's absolutely no evidence that
they are going crazy with their new freedoms, incidentally;
in fact, despite the surging stock market, still-conservative
Americans put a record net $102 billion into money-market
funds last year. Total money-market investments have
almost doubled in five years, providing a substantial cush-
ion against downturns.

All of this suggests not just continuing fuel for a bull
market that shows no signs of expiring, even now, but a
sense of independence that bodes well for another American century.

From "Let's Not Be Scared of Things That Go Bump in the Market"
—June 1998

Speaking of long-term investors, the young fellow at the bottom of this page goes straight to the head of the class. His photo was sent to me by his proud parents, Michelle and William Bors, of Upper Saddle River, N.J. And they claim he's strictly legit: "As you can see, our 18-month-old son Jack enjoys your newsletter. This picture was not staged—we actually caught him looking at it on his own! You may want to keep this picture. It could be worth something one day—who knows, he could be the next Warren Buffett!"

I don't doubt it for a minute. For the aptly named Jack has one great advantage over Warren Buffett, and all the rest of us to boot: he's starting younger. The magic of compound interest, and the miracle of long-term faith in the U.S. and its economic future, should work brilliantly for him and any of his contemporaries who share this vision. It used to be difficult to get people under 35 started in sensible investing: retirement seemed centuries off, a preoccupation only of doddering old folks of 50 or so, while the pressing needs of movies, cars, clothes, dates, vacations and similar absolute necessities were obvious and enticing.

Fortunately, the government has—inadvertently—been working for all of us. Its massive ineptness in dealing with the people's money is now so ubiquitous that only the most purblind statist could avoid the conclusion that private citizens cannot escape the task of doing their own financial planning. Oh, don't misunderstand me: the pooh-bahs of government-knows-best have not lost a shred of their traditional arrogance. We see this, for example, in their remarkable decision to wage all-out legal war on Microsoft, which apparently has committed the unforgivable crime of serving the American consumer too well. It's the latest of many recent evidences of the continuing demagogic war on success and the successful in America, based as usual on the implausible notion that government—which can't manage its own vast revenues even at the intelligence level of a bright 18-month-old—knows better than the marketplace what should be going on there. That there has never been any visible evidence of such governmental competency has never been a drawback to the political overreachers.

But little boys and girls are not as easy to fool as they used to be, and I suspect that in the 21st Century we will significantly reverse the trend toward ever-more-"redistributionist" tax policies and ever-more-intrusive governmental powers. The reasons are two, and both will become increasingly obvious to citizens at all economic

levels: the failures of government, and the successes of
private enterprise. Those who foresee this happy change
and pursue an optimistic long-term investing program are
going to be among the biggest winners of the century. I'm
betting on that entranced new reader, Jack Bors, to be
one of them.

From "Extra! Extra! Washington And Wall Street Wise Up"
—July 1998

The government's antitrust policy is a long-running bad joke, rooted in the discredited theories of a century ago and conspicuously ill-suited to the ultracompetitive world of the next century. It makes us an object of derision to overseas rivals, whose governments have not caught the spiteful academic disease of seeking to punish and retard a country's most successful enterprises. (We had the best telephone system in the world, so we waged war on AT&T. We had the finest computer company in the world, so we did battle with IBM. Now we're supposed to think it's just awful that Intel has become the world leader in semiconductors and Microsoft has shown the way in software. Lock 'em all up instantly!) In the Justice Department, of course, nothing succeeds like failure.

And so it is both stunning and heartening that a federal appeals court has so devastatingly rejected a central argument in the government's vendetta against Microsoft: that there was something reprehensible in the company's plan to insert its own browser (free) into Windows 98. As even the normally detached Federal Reserve chairman Alan Greenspan had tried to communicate, the record of antitrust legislation in seeking to improve competition suggests that there "ought to be a higher degree of humility." The market is faster, and smarter, than the professors.

I understand why Netscape and its allies are mad at

Number One; that goes with the territory. If they have a legal case, let them pursue it. But don't do it with taxpayer money and the arrogant power of the federal government. As a nation, we should cherish and encourage success, not least in the industry whose awesome products have done more to turn around the economy and raise our living standards than all the politicians and academic theorists combined. One cannot escape the conclusion that Microsoft's real sin, in the eyes of its tax-paid critics, was creating such magnificent progress without government authorization or regulation.

It's nice to see an influential court in agreement. Not only does this increase the possibility that the government will simply drop its latest ill-conceived cases and get out of the way of these splendid engines of American prosperity, but it presents us with a hopeful new standard for the future: beating your competitors by better serving the customer is not as un-American as we had been told.

From "Extra! Extra! Washington And Wall Street Wise Up"
—July 1998

The notion that the tax situation is purely a concern of the right-wing rich has always been nonsense. It was Jimmy Carter who described the convoluted U.S. tax code as "a disgrace to the human race," and that code is infinitely more complex and confusing today than it was two decades ago. The bipartisan move toward simplification in the mid-1980s foundered shamefully, leading to a series of changes from newly created tax brackets to newly invented categories of different kinds of interest to a capital-gains code so baffling that even the IRS couldn't figure out, for weeks last year, what the heck it really meant.

Now, finally, there are glimmers of hope. Perhaps the single dumbest thing the Treasury did last year (and that's always a heavily contested annual competition) was blocking an overdue reduction in capital-gains taxes until Congress agreed to limit the most-favorable rate to assets held for at least 18 months. The bureaucratic geniuses thus created still-another complication in the endless tax code; instead of the traditional division into short-term and long-term gains, we were now to have "medium-term" transactions as well, for assets held between 12 and 18 months. And, just for good measure, the tax writers threw in a bundle of other new distinctions, relating to different brackets and different kinds of investments.

In late June, Congressional negotiators agreed to two fundamental improvements: (1) the IRS will henceforth have to extend to innocent taxpayers at least a modicum of the constitutional protections the government routinely accords to rapists and murderers; and (2) the silly change in capital-gains holding periods will be repealed, returning the long-term requirement to anything over a year. (The notion of any required holding period at all should eventually disappear entirely, since it is based on the ludicrous assumption that the wastrels of Washington know better than you do how and when you should be investing your own money.) Even more encouragingly, this unaccustomed success in returning to at least minimal common sense is inspiring serious attention to other enduring flaws in the code, including the vindictive taxation of estates. In the immortal words of Steve Allen's only hit, "This could be the start of something big."

The point is not just that taxes are too darned high—though they certainly are: the Tax Foundation just reported that the U.S. burden has never previously been as high as it is today. The point is also that our ridiculously tangled tax code is an active impediment to good business. Individuals and corporations alike have to spend an inordinate amount of time (and money) calculating the tax implications of even the most routine economic and financial decisions. The tax code is an invisible participant who never leaves the room. This serves only two groups: the lawyers and accountants who are paid for guiding, tracking and unsnarling these decisions, and the politicians who get power—and contributions—because of their constant fiddling with the code. If there's truly some daylight coming up here, at last, all the rest of us should rejoice.

From "Economics 101: It's the Mood, Not the Mathematics"
—July 1998

One reason the professional economists of all persuasions have failed so miserably over the years in forecasting the economy is that they think they are dealing with a mathematical science. (Advanced economics courses these days are so heavily into abstruse numbers that they should probably be attended only by your computer.) In the real world, however, the very thing that makes these forecasts so fallible is precisely what makes life so interesting: the actual economy is made up of human beings, and they often don't behave the way the printouts say they should.

This is highly relevant to why the stock market has performed such miracles in recent years, and why, in my judgment, sensible investors should be planning for a continuance of those gains in the years ahead. For the academics tend habitually to underrate the importance of such intangibles as the national mood. Yet, as we have seen as recently as the start of this decade, when confidence evaporates, the economy can spiral downhill—far more steeply than the objective economic numbers would have suggested. And when optimism is more widespread, it can become a self-fulfilling prophecy.

Right now, for example, the U.S. economy plainly is decelerating: in part because of the reverberations from Asia's implosion and in part because of such internal policy errors as excessive taxation. This is showing up in some disappointing corporate earnings reports, notably in the industrial sector, and in several of the broader indicators as well. But the stock market has already had an impressive rebound from its late-spring selloff, and the fundamental reason is the relatively cheerful mood of individuals both in the economy and in the financial markets.

The American consumer is the authentic national hero these days. Consumer spending barreled ahead at a 6.1% annual rate in the first quarter (the speediest in a year), and while the overall economy has throttled back since then, consumer spending continues to be impressive: retail sales kept on advancing in April and May. Media hype about corporate downsizing has lost its sting in a high-employment economy, and it doesn't take a Ph.D. for the average family to figure out that the combination of rising incomes and stable prices ain't all bad. Asia? So far its chief effect in the typical American home has been to make imports cheaper. The dollar too strong? Ditto. Interest rates? Low and falling.

Not surprisingly, then, the retail and housing sectors have been the economy's stars of late. And a historically rewarding stock market not only reflects this improved national mood but contributes to it. (Just see how the ailing technology stocks sprang back to life on evidence that [A] maybe Americans would actually continue to buy a computer or two in the next decade, and [B] the government was being thwarted in at least some of its efforts to punish the success of leaders like Microsoft.)

Could it all end? Sure, but don't bet on it yet. Sales of

new homes set a record in April; May sales of existing homes came near one. The U.S. auto industry had its best sales in 11 years in May. The general economy is slowing from its brief recent growth spurt, but consumers still have plenty of money—and, perhaps even more important, plenty of confidence.

And one of the most significant places where they are reposing that confidence these days, with tens of billions of dollars of new money every month, is in equity mutual funds. Contrary to cynical predictions, these shareholders don't panic and flee every time the market tumbles (leave that to the laughably named "smart money"), they no longer buy politicians' assurances that Mama Government can be counted on to do the job for them, and they clearly believe that America's economic future is going to be better than its past. They won't always be right, but over the years that's a mood that will pay off handsomely for them— and for the country. ■

Louis Rukeyser

With

Other Financial Experts

Louis Rukeyser
With
Other Financial Experts

With Laszlo Birinyi

Let's say it simply and clearly: Laszlo Birinyi, Jr. is the single most on-target securities analyst operating in the 1990s. This will not come as startling news to readers of Louis Rukeyser's Wall Street, *who have been benefiting mightily from his brilliant stock selections in his annual appearances in the newsletter. Laszlo's stock-picking record on* Wall $treet Week With Louis Rukeyser *has long since become legendary; he is the #1 panelist by a wide margin over the five years ended December 31, 1997 (average annual gain: 44.3%). There comes a time when even the most dedicated "random walker" has to confess that this guy knows something the other guys don't.*

Born in Hungary, raised in Pennsylvania, Laszlo became Wall Street's finest number-cruncher before launching his own Greenwich, Conn., research and consulting firm, Birinyi Associates. He now manages more than $300 million for small businesses and individuals (minimum account: $2 million), but he gives his worthiest insights in Louis Rukeyser's Wall Street *every spring. And, by golly, we appreciate it.*

May 1996

Laszlo, as I noted when we talked a year ago, there have been only two kinds of market advisers in recent years: the pessimists and those who got it right. Yet, despite conspicuous exceptions like ourselves, what passes for financial advice in most of the media continues overwhelmingly downbeat. Indeed, some of the scare stories in major publications have become almost laughably repetitive—and perennially wrong. How do you explain this continuing bad guidance?

I hope this isn't the case, but I just wonder if perhaps journalists aren't to some degree ill-disposed toward the financial markets in general, and especially toward the people who work there. Or it could be that the negative case for the market is almost always more comprehensible, because the positive case is based upon the fact that the market discounts the future, and the market never really tells you what the good news *is* around the corner—while the bad news is always staring you in the face.

Given people's natural nervousness about money, they're always wondering when the next big selloff is going to come. What signs will you be looking for?

The one thing that has impressed me is that for all the discussion of mutual-fund purchases by individuals, more money last year went into money-market funds than into stock funds. When individuals start taking money out of their money-market funds to buy stocks, then to me the yellow light is on. But so far, people have not gotten carried away. When people get exuberant and are willing to mortgage their son's college tuition to buy stocks, then I think I'll look for a place to hide.

Finally, what's your best advice now to serious, long-term investors?

Don't watch the market! The day-to-day movements that we've seen this year are very unnerving, even to the professionals. Recognize that you are indeed making a long-term investment, and Wall Street loves to create a great deal of noise to shake your faith in that investment and to make money for itself. In the 25 years I've been on Wall Street, one thing I've learned is that the purpose of Wall Street is to make money for Wall Street, not for its customers.

Is there a simple basis for your long-term bullishness?

All the historical work I've ever seen says that common stocks are the economic manifestation of belief in the future. And as long as companies keep coming out with new products, innovations, technological changes and upgrades to our lifestyle, the best way to take advantage of this is in the stocks of those companies.

With Susan Byrne

Susan Byrne says her cautious approach to investing comes from having watched markets gyrate over the past quarter century, since she began at the bottom as appointments secretary to a brokerage-firm CEO. She quickly showed that she was destined for greater things, and by 1983 had started her own firm, Westwood Management Corporation, with offices in Dallas and New York. But the truly remarkable thing about Susan is not that she knows how to run scared; it's how much money she picks up for her clients along the track.

Not only do her Westwood Equity and Westwood Balanced funds (both available through Gabelli Funds, 800-937-8966, along with her smaller Westwood Intermediate Bond Fund) consistently shine in their respective performance categories, but Susan has proved an even-more-sensational stock-picker for readers of my newsletters. Clearly, this lady has more than good balance on her side.

December 1996

Susan, you've been remarkably on target for our readers with your predictions, both for the overall market and for individual stocks. What are you doing that most of your competitors are missing?

Well, we're not momentum players: we don't need a stock to be acting well for us to find it attractive. We just do good old fundamental research, and we don't pay that much attention to emotion. We're not afraid to own things that aren't popular.

What is the key test you use in picking securities for your funds?

We're looking to buy growth cheaply—which sounds like an impossibility in this market, but it's really not. We're trying to buy growth at a price/earnings ratio that is only 75% of the rate at which we think the company will grow. The key word there is what *we* think, not what the market thinks. As that growth comes through, and other people's confidence moves up, you generally get an expansion in the P/E, and that's where we usually make our money.

You have emphasized that you believe strongly in lowering risk, even if this means sacrificing some gains. You have said you want to capture 80% or 90% of the market's gains and avoid 30% to 50% of its declines. Sounds great— but how do you implement this strategy?

My favorite metaphor is baseball. To put a baseball team together, you have to have more than a pitcher. Somebody has to catch the ball. Somebody has to bat cleanup—maybe they play right field, they're not a very good fielder. You don't look for the guy who's the short-stop to bat cleanup, but he has to be able to field. You see what I mean? When you put a portfolio together, we don't have the same aspirations for everything that gets in there. When we put the whole portfolio together, hope-fully it's a team, each of which is doing its job. Some things in the portfolio, such as our REITs [real estate investment trusts], are there to produce yield, to soften the volatility. Clearly, *Dell* is in there for capital appreciation, and that is its sole job. That's how we try to accomplish our aims with the least amount of volatility— even though sometimes my analysts say, "Oh, you always sound so negative. Look at our returns."

Does it embarrass you that you're doing so well?

[laughs] Well, no! I work with a great group of people, and I'm not embarrassed to be doing well. I'm grateful to be doing well. But we're always focusing on the long run.

Do you deliberately seek out Wall Street's orphans?

No, but it happens that way when you're trying to find the best growth at the lowest price. I don't get involved in stocks just to be contrary—you don't get performance by just being contrary—but I am looking for companies where we're seeing something that maybe somebody else isn't seeing, and we can buy that growth cheaply.

What makes you decide to sell a stock, and what's your typical turnover?

Our typical turnover would be somewhere between 50% and 70% a year; that would include some bonds too, in the case of the Balanced fund. We sell, basically, for two reasons: the stock reaches its price objective (which we target as [the P/E] being in excess of the company's growth rate) or something changes at the company that we don't really understand. We also will sell if we buy a stock and it goes down 15% on us in the first month; it's better to admit the error real fast.

Finally, Susan, what's your single best piece of advice for investors over the next 12 months?

Stay invested. The best thing that's happened to me is that I've been much too busy to switch my own IRA around, and I've just kept it invested. Just set your goal and get good funds and stick with them. If you've got the right people, they'll do the worrying for you.

With Bill Miller

The name on his birth certificate is William H. Miller III,
but to his pals he's just plain Bill. Don't let Bill Miller's
simple stress on old-fashioned value investing fool you,
though. Not only does he interpret that style in a highly
personal way, as you'll see below, but he brings a unique
philosophical slant to the job of investing billions of dollars
for Legg Mason, including two top-performing mutual
funds (800-577-8589): Special Investment and the flagship
Value Trust—a highly ranked member of The Rukeyser 100
in Louis Rukeyser's Mutual Funds.

The veteran money manager doubles as a board member
of the Santa Fe Institute, which studies similarities within
complex systems like economics, ecology and the body's
immune system. One of the institute's principal conclusions
is that systems adapt to their environments, and thus histo-
ry does not always repeat itself. Bill told me that such theo-
retical work "has been surprisingly helpful with respect to
the stock market." For some other original conclusions
from one of the market's deftest practitioners, read on.

February 1997

Bill, your investment style seems to confuse some people. You call yourself a
value manager, but your holdings often strike others as tipping over into the
growth area. What is your approach to investing?

Our approach has been consistent for the 15 years that I've been managing the Legg Mason Value Trust: we look for quality companies with excellent managements at bargain prices. Some people believe that companies that are growing can't represent good value. We think this is a false dichotomy.

What are the key tests you use in picking stocks?

We're trying to buy companies at large discounts to our assessment of their underlying value. We use a multi-factor valuation approach. At one level it's highly theoretical: we look at the present value of the future free-cash flows of the business, and that gives us one kind of a number. We also look at the liquidation value, the private market value, and historical and prospective valuations—things like price/earnings and price-to-book and price-to-cash-flow. All those things together give us a central tendency of valuation. And if that as a price is considerably above what the company is trading at, then we like to buy it. We like to buy hysteria and sell euphoria.

Which are we nearer to right now?

Well, contrary to the pessimists—who tend to change their view every year about why the market's going to do poorly—we actually think that the market is fairly valued right now. There's no sign that the economic expansion is going to end any time soon; all the components point to a year of moderate expansion with low inflation.

And we think interest rates will likely be moderately higher at worst.

Bill, as you've suggested, you use a number of highly mathematical methods for picking your stocks. Do they sometimes lead you astray? Do you sometimes have to override them with the seat of your pants?

Well, this central tendency we identify gets us in the valuation ballpark. But then we do a careful analysis of business fundamentals: company prospects, what the products are like, what the management's like—importantly, how they allocate capital—and what their competitive position is. So the balance to the valuation is an assessment of business fundamentals.

You have notably low turnover in Value Trust; you tend to hold stocks for five years or longer. What makes you decide to sell?

We sell when one of three things happens: the company approaches our fair-value target; we find a better bargain; or our investment case is no longer applicable—that is to say, when we find that we're wrong about a company.

A fellow with your very long-term perspective must always be looking for new trends. What do you see as the next important trends for which investors should be watching?

Perhaps the most interesting is the decline of economic volatility. Most people have a view of the economy, and therefore the market, as cyclical: we've had a history of having recessions and bear markets every three to four years. But the economic picture in the U.S. has changed, and we've only had eight months of recession in the last 15 years. Now we've had two very long expansions that bracket each side of that.

And if you look at the trends in volatility—in inflation, for example, and in economic growth and short-term interest rates—all are declining. Declining volatility means higher justifiable P/E ratios. We think valuations are in a broad shift that will benefit companies that will be less affected by the business cycle.

What's the most important lesson you have learned as an investor?

Focus on the long term, ignore interim fluctuations, concentrate on buying good-quality companies at bargain prices—and let the market take care of itself. We have very little truck with the pessimists who are always looking for reasons why the market is going to decline or why things are going to go wrong. The market almost always goes up; it goes up two-thirds of the years, two-thirds of the months and even two-thirds of the days.

But at least two-thirds of the media commentators are always pessimistic.

It certainly seems that way. I wrote in my shareholder letter that will be going out soon that I think the pessimists suffer from the disorder that the psychologists call "simultanagnosia," which is a term that refers to the ability to pick out parts and features of things that suit your purposes, but be unable to integrate anything into a meaningful whole. And that's what I think the pessimists do.

With Ralph Acampora

Nobody in the business is more serious about the alchemy known as "technical market analysis" than my longtime friend and television panelist Ralph Acampora. Indeed, we first met two decades ago when Ralph invited me to speak at a meeting of the group he co-founded in 1970, the Market Technicians' Association—a sort of Institute for Advanced Studies for elves. As I said to the group then, and have reiterated in these pages, the problem with most technicians is that their impressively arcane formulas can be relied on only when tomorrow turns out to be precisely like yesterday. Which, alas for them, rarely happens.

Ironically, as you'll see below, Ralph has come at least partially to share this view—and he regards overreliance on past patterns as the trap that turned the majority of both chartists and quantitative analysts ("quants") into conspicuous wrong-way bears. He scored a forecasting triumph of his own in 1997 by recognizing that something actually was different this time around.

March 1997

Ralph, when you first predicted on *Wall Street Week With Louis Rukeyser* in July 1995 that the Dow Jones Industrial Average would hit 7000 by the start of 1998, many people thought you were a cockeyed optimist. In fact, the

Dow reached that target nearly a year earlier. Have we come too far too fast, or are you raising your sights?

I'm raising my sights—because I think my original thesis is too conservative. When the market stays in a wide trading range, quant models identifying "overvaluation" and "undervaluation," and technical oscillators looking for "overbought" and "oversold" readings, work. But once a generation, Lou, you come into what we call a "secular-trending market." And what that means is that the market keeps climbing and climbing, and all the indicators we created in the oscillating days—the quant models and the technical models—don't work. They're the right tools for the wrong market.

And what I did was go back to the last period when we had such a change: 1962 to 1966. I read every *Wall Street Journal* for four years. And I realized that we were experiencing, for the first time in more than 30 years, a similar environment of low inflation and low interest rates. So I thought the trend would last as long as it did in the early '60s. Since we're getting to my target a year early, that tells me that maybe it's going to be more like the '50s than the '60s, and that I was too conservative about this move.

I don't want to oscillate with you, Ralph, but when you talk about interest rates and inflation, that sounds dangerously like fundamental analysis to me.

Oh, sure. I also think the market's telling us that there's a revolution going on in our government and that, before it's over, they are going to balance the budget. That's insane for a technician to say—but I'm trying to create a reason behind the strength I see.

OK. How high are you targeting now?

I think we'll get to 8250 [in 1997]—and that is subject to an upward revision, believe it or not. First, because the market leadership is so strong; when you have Procter & Gamble and Philip Morris and General Electric making new highs, that's great stuff. Second, because of the liquidity supplied by the Baby Boomers—every seven-and-a-half seconds, someone in this country is turning 50—plus the strength of the dollar, which attracts foreign investors. Third, I like to be contrarian—especially to other technicians.

Why do you think so many of your fellow technical analysts have been so consistently and incorrectly bearish about this market's historic duration and strength?

Because very few of them have made the switch from an oscillating market to a trending market, Lou. I'm not going to get off this trend until I see something negative happen—such as much more speculation than we have seen so far.

Suppose interest rates were to rise.

That's the big caveat, Lou. The killer would be if we had rising rates. I could live with [long-term rates of] 7% or even 7.25%, which we did last year, but if you honestly believe that we're going to 8% or 9%, all bets are off.

One of the things that seem to worry many market skeptics is what they regard as excessive bullishness. Could they be right?

No, they're wrong. The other day, when we crossed 7000, the ratio of bulls to bears among market-letter writers actually declined—to only 49% bullish. That means that as we're going higher, people are saying, "Well, this has got to be the end." So, no, no, no—sentiment is not overly bullish. When I ask portfolio managers around the country why they're in the market, they say because they have to be, not because they want to be; most of their personal portfolios are in cash. So I say most people are chicken bulls.

What kind of a hybrid is that?

[laughs] One that makes me feel very, very happy! But the market's not going to go straight up. Later this year or early next year, I think we'll have a bear market—20% to 25% on the downside. But between now and then, belly up to the bar; you got to be there.

And then after the bear market?

I've jokingly said, "When we make the bottom in 1998, I'm going to come out and say, 'Back the truck up to the front door and buy anything with a symbol.'" I think it'll set the stage, Lou, for a huge upward move going into the new millennium.

With Ralph Wanger

Ralph Wanger marches to a different drummer—toy-size variety. Rather than keeping in step with the crowd's changing tempos, his Acorn Fund (800-922-6769; no load) finds its rhythms in an individualistic search for quirky, small and often-obscure companies that fit into the societal trends he discerns. Ralph's long-term record is superb; not coincidentally, the fund's assets have swelled, and Ralph and his team also manage Acorn International (all invested outside the U.S.) and a new, more-concentrated U.S. small-stock fund, Acorn USA.

A native of Chicago, where he now runs Wanger Asset Management, Ralph took two degrees at M.I.T. before launching an investment career unusual both for its durability and its iconoclasm. Professional money managers surveyed by USA Today in 1994 voted him the investment professional whom they would most like to manage their own money. But Ralph maintains a sense of humor about his accomplishments, as you'll see below and in his Simon & Schuster book, A Zebra in Lion Country. Clearly, he has earned his stripes.

June 1997

Ralph, the comeback of the small-stock sector has been one of the most predicted events of this decade. What has been stopping it, and when can we really expect to see it?

The first thing that's been stopping it has been a very good rate of earnings growth by large-cap companies, which has made them fashionable and attracted money, and it's become sort of a self-fulfilling cycle. But small-cap companies are doing well as a group, and with the dollar being strong this year—as opposed to weak last year—big companies with export businesses may have some negative comparisons. But I would guess the major turn will be after the next bear market.

Are you expecting that real soon?

No. I don't know when it's going to come, but if you look at when major cycles of small-cap outperformance have started, they've started after we have had a general washout.

While the Acorn Fund outperformed its contemporaries last year, its three-year record has trailed a bit. Was this because of your penchant for foreign small stocks?

That was only a minor hurt; they've kept up fairly well. We held some cable-TV and gaming stocks too long. But '96 and so far in '97 have been just fine.

Have you learned something from that uncharacteristic two-year lag?

The first thing you learn is that you can't win 'em all. Second, we learned that when these stocks start underperforming, we should take a sharp critical look a little earlier than we did last time. I hope we'll make a different mistake next time!

You're famous for combining a look at the numbers with a broader look at what's going on throughout society. How do you set about the task of picking stocks?

We try to keep our turnover low. Trading costs on small-cap stocks are extremely high. We cut costs by not trading; we're very concerned about keeping taxes down. Acorn's turnover rate (between 20% and 35% for the last decade) is one of the lowest in our peer group. You'll find many funds whose annual turnover is 100% or higher.

But if you hold stocks for the long term, you need to have a reason to believe that they have a long-term advantage over the rest of the market. So you become a theme investor: you try to find something that's going on in the economy that is going to favor a specific group.

What are some of the themes you're playing now?

I'm very impressed by the amount of outsourcing and privatization that is going on in Europe, and I think this is a trend that will spread to the U.S. Europe, which had more government-owned facilities—and therefore more trouble—has been privatizing, downsizing and outsourcing much more rapidly than the U.S. For instance, the airports in Europe are run by private businesses, which is just starting in the U.S. We see a lot of opportunities coming from this trend, because there really are few government services that can't be handled more efficiently by private business.

If you could find a private business that would take over the White House and Congress, would you invest in it?

Well, Clinton has done fairly well at privatizing the
White House: making a bed-and-breakfast out of it is quite
in concert with this sort of theme. So I think he, as usual,
is well ahead of society in this matter.

Since you're such a specialist in themes, Ralph, tell us the main theme of *A
Zebra in Lion Country.*
The main theme is that investors act in terms of
metaphor—they don't do it as economists or mathemati-
cians. We all like metaphors, we investors: "The stock
will be another Home Depot" is a sort of metaphor. So I'm
trying to take a philosophic look at the investing process:
an investing theme is really a metaphoric way of looking
at the world.

**Speaking of the world, you're obviously more interested in overseas invest-
ments than the average U.S. shareholder is. Why do you think there has been
so much resistance?**
Well, it's certainly true that most U.S. investors are
underinvested outside the U.S. The U.S. in terms of world
stock-market weightings is only about 40%—so if you had
60% of your investments outside the U.S., you'd match the
world. But I'd say that trying to get people to make it 20%
or 30% is about as aggressive as I can be without being
treated as a madman.

Americans *have* increased the amount they have outside
the U.S.—from 5% to 10%—and that's been a nice
increase over the last few years. In 1993, a year of enthusiasm for foreign stocks, an enormous slug of money came

into the funds. But, as happens after all enthusiasms, there was a sobering-up period in '94 and '95 when these markets were very poor. So a lot of people got in at the top and were disappointed the next couple of years; comparing these results with a strong U.S. market, they figured, "Well, I guess the foreigners don't know how to make any money." And that discouraged people for a while.

You said a revival of real enthusiasm for U.S. small stocks might have to await another bear market. Do you think it would take a bear market in the U.S. to increase enthusiasm for foreign stocks, too?

No. A bear market might just dissuade people from stocks anyplace. Very few people would say, "Well, I'm losing money in the U.S.—I think I'll try Thailand." But what would help would be better relative performance by foreign markets. Diversification is much more salable when it's profitable diversification.

With L. Keith Mullins

*Any parent who has been nonplussed by the behavior of a trou-
blesome teenager (could we have a show of hands, please?)
should have sympathy for L. Keith Mullins, who has long
been one of Wall Street's leading authorities on "emerging
growth" stocks. To Keith, that represents the adolescent stage
of corporate development: the company is no longer a privately held baby, but it's far from mature. Traditionally,
investors have been appropriately rewarded for taking on the
extra risk of dealing with these volatile creatures. Lately,
however, most of the money has been gravitating toward
larger, more-established companies. On Wall Street in the
1990s, less has not been more.*

*With many strategists believing that a change is at
hand, and that emerging companies now deserve a heftier
share in the average portfolio, it seemed timely to talk again
with Keith, who has been specializing in the area for more
than a dozen years and has been on the Institutional
Investor All-America Research Team since 1988.*

July 1997

**Keith, slower growth has historically been a good environment for smaller
companies, hasn't it?**

It's been terrific. The last time I really made a lot of
money was 1991—and, as you know, that's when corporate

profitability took it on the chin. If in fact we get a similar environment to 1991, I think we can make an awful lot of money in the smaller stocks.

Does an investor in smaller companies have to have a different temperament than an investor in the big blue chips?

Almost exactly the opposite. If you make a mistake in a small stock and the stock drops 30%, you should sell it, generally, because the odds are enormously stacked that the company will continue to be a disappointment—whereas in a big stock, if it drops 30%, the company usually has the resources to work itself out of the problem. Similarly, if you get a small stock that works, and the business continues to deliver and surprise, you should hold on to it. The temptation is to sell something that's up 30% or so and add to those stocks that have come down. You'll lose a lot of money that way.

Given your view that mistakes in smaller companies are much more serious than mistakes in larger companies, is that itself an argument for diversification in this group?

If you don't diversify, you'd better have a pretty good medical plan! If you're not able to buy a dozen stocks, buy a mutual fund. It's just not practical to try to rifle-shoot this industry.

With Ron Canakaris

Ronald E. Canakaris has always been remarkably consistent—and the good news is that he is now cheap, too. As the steward of Enterprise Growth Fund since 1980, Ron is one of the very few fund managers who have beaten the S&P 500 over the short and long runs. But Enterprise Growth A shares carry a sales charge of 4.75%. What hasn't been widely publicized is that since Dec. 1, 1994, Ron has been offering an absolutely identical portfolio, with no sales charge, under the name of Montag & Caldwell Growth Fund. At the same time, he launched Montag & Caldwell Balanced Fund, which also has been smartly outperforming its peers (both: 800-992-8151; no load).

Small wonder, then, that Montag & Caldwell Growth already has more assets than the older Enterprise Growth. Ron, who joined Atlanta-based Montag & Caldwell in 1972 and has been president and chief investment officer since 1984, has been showing his acuity in other ways, too: he has done even better picking stocks for my newsletters than for his high-flying funds.

October 1997

Ron, this has clearly been your kind of market, with the great global titans leading the way. Now we hear a lot of talk about smaller companies emerging as the new market leaders. Do you see this happening, and if so how, if at all, will it affect your own investment style?

Well, if they're good small companies, I think they'll do fine. But I certainly wouldn't exchange the opportunity to be global for anything. As you exit this period where you've had a very strong economy, and as corporate-profit growth becomes more moderate over the next six months, I think the best global companies' growth rates will compare very favorably to corporate-profit growth in general.

So you don't see the trend changing over the long haul.

No, I don't. The recent pullback in some of these stocks occurred because they got fully priced, and there was some moderation in their growth, while at the same time overall corporate-profit growth was better than expected. But this pullback has resulted in some attractive valuation levels in our work—so now you have both good relative earnings-strength prospects and better valuations.

What are the key things you look for in choosing stocks for your funds?

Our first criterion is that the companies show strong secular earnings-growth rates, above 10%. We want earnings momentum. But we also want these stocks to be reasonably priced. By combining earnings growth with price, we've been able to buy stocks at the right price at the right time.

We rank all the data in order for all the stocks we're considering, from the most attractive to the least attractive. We want to buy stocks at a discount to what we consider their intrinsic value—or the present value of their future stream of income. We also rank earnings momentum, in terms of intermediate-term earnings growth; we want this momentum to be above-average.

How far ahead do you think you can accurately predict earnings growth?

In the intermediate term, we're looking at six to 12 months. But we also try to value a company's longer-term growth prospects, and there we're using a five- to 10-year horizon.

The course of interest rates is critical to the price/earnings ratios that growth stocks command. Do you have an interest-rate forecast?

We do. We think bond yields will be steady to lower, because we see the outlook for inflation as being quite good. With real bond yields now in excess of 400 basis points [four percentage points], we think bonds are mispriced. As investors gain confidence that lower-inflation policies are here to stay, bond yields will move lower.

Would this make you become even more aggressive in buying stocks?

Well, it certainly will support and enhance shareholder value, because you'll be able to pay more now for a dollar of future earnings. And that, Lou, actually has much more effect on valuations than a change in the growth rate in earnings. A decline in interest rates of one percentage point will enhance the normal valuation of stocks, particularly growth stocks, by 17% to 20%—whereas a one-percentage-point change in our expected earnings for a company over a 10-year period would change the normalized valuation by just 10%. So we think steady-to-lower bond yields will prove far more important for the market than stronger-than-anticipated profit growth.

You sound pretty optimistic.

Lou, we think the outlook right now is probably the best it's been in our lifetime. We have a combination of a very good policy mix, rapidly improving technology and globalization of trade. This suggests sustained growth in the economy and corporate profits, with low inflation.

What could go wrong?

A policy error, or some movement away from the globalization of trade. But I think those developments are not likely. I do think it's important that the Federal Reserve let this momentum toward lower inflation play itself out, and not overreact—because by definition you could then have deflation as a problem. With inflation close to zero, you wouldn't want to see an unnecessary decline in the economy. But so far, so good.

Ron, while your emphasis is on global competitiveness, most of your holdings are U.S. companies. Is this by design?

Yes. These companies, on average, derive about 40% of their sales from global markets. So here we've got companies that are very high-quality, that trade very well, and whose accounting we clearly understand. We think this is the way to participate in global markets.

Ron, a conventional view, particularly among those who have been totally wrong about the course of this historic bull market, is that popular growth stocks such as yours are ridiculously overpriced and are heading for a disastrous fall. Are they ever going to be right?

[laughs] Well, maybe if these stocks eventually did get real overpriced—but that's not showing up in our work. This is a real good question, Lou, because investors tend to look back only to times of high inflation. If they look further back, to such periods of sustained low inflation as the 1960s, I think they'll reach a different conclusion about valuations. And what I think is going to happen is that, as bond yields decline, good growth stocks are going to go to valuations that will be higher than investors expect.

With Spiros (Sig) Segalas

In a business where investing flashes come and go with each passing quarter, and where anybody with a system that seems to work for more than two weeks straight immediately claims a spot on the Internet, Sig Segalas has the genuine—and rare—expertise that reflects not just his outstanding intelligence and acumen but the seasoned wisdom that has grown through a 37-year investing career.

As further evidence of the value of such a background, Sig's Harbor Capital Appreciation Fund (800-422-1050; no load) has been so consistently successful under his stewardship since 1990 that it regularly appears in the Long-Term-Growth category of The Rukeyser 100 in Louis Rukeyser's Mutual Funds. *Such sustained excellence is even more remarkable since the fund has never been known for playing it safe in the market's less-volatile sectors. Sig is no "closet indexer"; he makes big, bold and historically successful bets.*

December 1997

Sig, congratulations on another fine year. What are you doing that your competitors are failing to do?

I don't think we're doing anything different than we've done in the past. We just try to buy attractively priced growth stocks, basically in the large-cap arena, and buy them at the right time. For a long time, I've tended to have 20% to 40% of the assets in technology stocks, and that clearly has helped us this year on balance. But starting in July, after the group had run up quite a bit, I cut back a little, just to get our holdings in this area down to a more prudent level—though I still have about 29% in technology; it's one of the few true growth industries around.

Stocks in general, notably including those in the technology sector, were shaken by the troubles that began in Asia in October. Have you made any significant changes as a result of those events?

Well, I must confess, the Asian situation has me concerned, if for no other reason than I don't think we truly understand the implications of what's going on in that part of the world. A lot of our incremental growth, and not just in technology, has come from Asia. But my portfolio hasn't changed that much. I've bought a little more in the domestic area, but I still like my multinationals; I think the market has already adjusted for a number of the earnings concerns.

How do you assess the outlook for 1998?

My guess is that the market will back and fill for the rest of 1997, which would not be all that bad: the market's up nicely this year, and before the recent correction it was fully priced, on a short-term basis. The Asian situation was the catalyst for some people to take profits. But that Asian situation takes away the risk of a synchronized world recovery, which was one of the concerns people had. What this means to me is that inflation will continue to behave well—if not surprise on the downside—and this bodes very well for interest rates. So while I think we have a somewhat higher risk of earnings disappointments (though I expect overall increases of 8% to 10%), interest rates are going to be coming down, which is very good for stocks. On balance, I think the market next year will be up about 10%.

Your willingness to buy highly volatile stocks, such as those in the technology sector, has occasionally given your shareholders a bumpy ride for a while, when those stocks go into one of their periodic nosedives. Do you need strong nerves to invest in your fund?

I don't think so, but you have to be a long-term investor. I'm basically a large-cap manager, and the companies I invest in— even though they get bumpy, as you put it, once in a while— always are sure to come back. They tend to be leaders in their marketplaces, with very strong financials and very strong balance sheets.

While many large-cap-growth managers pay attention to earnings momentum, and you have told me it is "very important" to you, you always have wanted to look beyond the raw numbers to see what was producing that momentum. Why don't you give us an example of how you analyze an individual company in this respect.

One thing I'm very sensitive to is top-line growth—that is, I want to see revenue growth, not just margin improvements created by cutting costs. At some point, that game runs out. And I want companies whose revenue growth comes more from unit sales than price increases, which are short-lived (and harder to implement in the present environment). Compaq, for example, shows up well because its unit growth is better than 50%, which means it can cut prices, broaden the market and maintain its margins.

Give me an example of a company that looks pretty good on the bottom line but not on the top—one that you wouldn't buy for that reason.

Well, I may even buy it! [laughs] United Technologies is cheap, with a management committed to earnings growth of 15%—but top-line growth of only 3% or 4%. The stock may do fine in an environment where people gravitate toward earnings predictability, but I just haven't convinced myself how long that 15% growth can persist if the top line's only 3% or 4%. That would suggest huge margin improvement.

What makes you decide to sell a stock?

One reason is the obvious one: there's a mistake, and you want to get out. But apart from that, as stocks reach our price targets I like to shave the position—not get out entirely; that's being too smart—but if the fundamentals are still there, I'll just do some cutting back on strength. And finally, as a matter of discipline, I like to have no more than about 60 stocks in the portfolio, which means that if I want to buy a new name that I'm very enthusiastic about, I have to sell something—and seven out of 10 times I end up selling something I should have sold in the first place.

What's your best advice to investors for the next 12 months?

Dollar-averaging [regular infusions of new cash into the same investments] is always the best advice, especially in the volatile markets we're in. And I think you should have a diversified portfolio: a growth fund like mine, and maybe an international fund and even a small-cap fund. But be somewhat diversified in any case; don't put all your money in one fund. And to the degree possible, I would dollar-average—and hang in there.

With Sir John Templeton

The world is not just John Templeton's oyster, it is his mission. In the strictly financial sense, it is he who has prodded Americans for 57 years not to let their investing horizons stop at the border. In the spiritual sense, it is he who for 25 years has funded the nonsectarian Templeton Prize for Progress in Religion, the world's largest philanthropic monetary award. Central to his beliefs, and to his life, has been the often-unfashionable idea that free enterprise not only is in no way the enemy of humane values but is, in fact, its true best friend.

Sir John, as this 85-years-young dynamo is known to Queen Elizabeth and his neighbors in the Bahamas, has been technically retired for five years, since he sold (and severed all ties with) the Templeton mutual funds. But, as you'll see below, his brain is as crisp as when he moved from Winchester, Tenn., to Yale to a Rhodes Scholarship at Oxford more than six decades ago. He is an old friend of mine (a record 15 appearances on Wall $treet Week With Louis Rukeyser, *charter membership in its Hall of Fame) and of my newsletters, where his regular appearances over the years have offered exclusive opportunities to find out the latest thinking of one of the century's most incisive— and kindest—minds.*

January 1998

John, the title of your newest thought-provoking book is, "Is Progress Speeding Up?" What's the answer to that question, and what does it portend both financially and spiritually?

The answer is yes, and we should be overwhelmingly grateful, Louis. Because the media live on bad news, we get brainwashed into thinking we're in a period of difficulty, when we're living in the most glorious period in all world history in almost every area you look at. We should be thankful every morning to be living in this time. The amount of information that's discovered now is doubling every three years, so progress over the next generation, and the next century, will be even more rapid than it has been in the past.

By today's standards, mutual funds were small and embryonic when you first became involved with them. Now they are the investment of choice for a substantial percentage of the American population. Some believe that this is a dangerous trend, that these inexperienced investors will not understand or withstand a genuine bear market. What's your thinking on that?

It's true that there are millions of people who never invested before and have only lived through this 10-year bull market, and they will be upset when the next bear market arrives. And I predict there will be a major bear market in almost every nation at least once, probably twice, each 10 years. But I believe that mutual funds remediate the problem; they're not likely to pick as many bad stocks as the public would if they had to invest without the funds.

What would be your best advice to investors in mutual funds?
I'd subscribe to the Louis Rukeyser newsletters!

[laughs] John, we may have to make you chairman of the marketing committee!
Quite seriously, Louis, The Rukeyser 100 [a list of top-performing no- and low-load funds that appears each month in *Louis Rukeyser's Mutual Funds*] is an excellent tool. And other services like Morningstar and Value Line attempt to do the same thing. A person should subscribe to these services and buy the funds that have the maximum performance over a period of years.

Let's get back to your own thoughts on investing, John. One of your enduring convictions has been that as democracy spreads, inflation is inevitable. But today many people are becoming concerned that the new problem may be deflation and recession. Are they right?
Only temporarily. In the long run I would not favor Treasuries. It's just when share prices are higher than normal that I would recommend putting up to one-third of a person's total assets into, say, five-year Treasury STRIPs as a precaution, while you're waiting for the next bear market in America.

John, as we speak, critics of open capitalism are again becoming increasingly vocal in societies as diverse as Russia and Malaysia. Are you worried that the tide toward economic freedom may reverse?

Only in those nations that never had communism—
nations like America, which don't really understand the
horror of communism or of adopting policies that are
socialistic. The nations that lived under communism are
throwing out the Communists at each election.

Is it getting easier or harder to remain one of the world's most convinced optimists?
Easier and easier. Anybody who takes the time to exam-
ine it ought to be, every day, just overwhelmingly thankful
and grateful and joyful.

With Mike Holland

Michael F. Holland was a scrappy little running back for Harvard in the mid-1960s, and that competitive spirit has sustained him well in his impressive charge through Wall Street's upper echelons, scoring in top jobs at (among an array of prestigious others) J.P. Morgan, First Boston, Salomon Brothers, Oppenheimer and the Blackstone Group. But the truly amazing thing about Mike is that, after all those years in the headiest arenas of the financial industry, he still has so much common sense.

The clue to that, and to his sustained record of wise advice to individual investors, may lie in his more-recent athletic preoccupation: Mike runs marathons. A fellow who has completed those long-distance events from New York to London, from Boston to Paris, clearly has the patience, strategic thinking and endurance that are the bases of most investing achievements, too. As viewers of his frequent television appearances as a panelist on Wall $treet Week With Louis Rukeyser *are fondly aware, Mike has correctly kept the faith on this historically changed market, while others periodically faltered and panicked. Just the degree of cool one would expect of a fellow who, with wife Louise, has raised six sons. Professionally, Mike has been out on his own since 1995 as founder of New York's Holland & Co., where his expertise is now available to mutual-fund investors through the Holland Balanced*

Fund (800-304-6552; no load). Typically, it's geared to those who share Mike's enthusiasm for the long run.

February 1998

Mike, even by its own notoriously neurotic standards, the stock market has had a conflicted start in 1998. What's going on, and how do you think it will be resolved?

Well, Lou, this is just a continuation of the nervousness that has characterized this bull market from the get-go—and has kept securities prices from getting to genuinely speculative levels. Many U.S. investors, particularly institutional investors, continue to look for something to go bump in the night. But I believe we remain firmly in the midst of a golden era in financial history, which future generations will look back on with awe. People have trouble simply acknowledging, and taking advantage of, this incredible period. And, ironically, their jitteriness itself causes the whole thing to be prolonged.

You've spent a lot of time in Asia, and you're on the board of the closed-end China Fund. Give us a road map of what to expect in the Orient this year, and how much it is really going to impact the U.S. economy and individual companies.

I was in Hong Kong in December, and came away thinking that despite all the scare headlines, a number of positive outcomes are already identifiable. First and foremost, the American consumer is the direct beneficiary of lower-priced goods. Second, this downward pressure on prices has helped produce lower interest rates on auto and house loans. Third, while there will be pressure on earnings and sales for American companies operating in the so-called Asian tigers, this effect has been overstated: less than 9% of U.S. exports go to the affected countries, while fully 55% go to Europe, whose economies are looking up, and already offsetting the declines in Asia.

Asia's long-term strength, moreover, remains enormous; smart U.S. companies have recognized this and are taking advantage of the opportunity to invest cheaply right now. Anyone who has a three- to five-year view of the other side of the world will find major earnings strength reappearing there.

What's your best advice to investors for the next 12 months?

Every time the U.S. stock market gets as scary as it did last April and last October, use that as an incredible opportunity to buy extremely high-quality goods at distressed prices.

With Gary Haubold

Little things mean a lot to Gary Haubold—as those who have invested with him over the years are profitably aware. In the three-and-a-half years before he moved from Miller, Anderson & Sherrerd to Pilgrim, Baxter & Associates at the end of 1996, his two MAS mutual funds, Small-Cap Value and Mid-Cap Value, soundly trounced both the S&P 500 and (by even more impressive margins) the typical funds in their areas. Gary began his investing career equipped with an engineering degree from Rice and an MBA from Wharton, and he has specialized in building his own methodology: a disciplined blend of traditional "value" and "growth" approaches. From 1986 to 1993, he honed his asset-management skills at Wood, Struthers & Winthrop. Today, still in his early 40s, he has already engineered a personal spot near the top of the investment ladder.

March 1998

Gary, the comeback of the smaller stocks has been one of the most-predicted (and least-seen) phenomena of recent years. Yet your funds have somehow managed to make big money even when the sector lagged. What are you doing right?

Picking good stocks. I have a multifactor methodology that makes good tradeoffs between valuation and what you get in return—in terms of growth-rate estimate revisions, earnings surprises and a lot of attributes that investors value highly. There's more room for intelligent stock selection and stock jockeying in small-cap than there is in large-cap; while the S&P 500 is dominated by 100 or 120 of the largest blue-chip stocks, in small-cap investing there are literally 3,000 or 4,000 companies to choose from—and I need only 150 of the most-mispriced, most-attractive stocks to make up my portfolio.

To what extent do you rely on the quantitative data produced by your computers, and to what extent do you factor in your own human insight?

It's approximately half and half. Stock-market performance is determined by what happens in the real world on a fundamental-business basis. And while the computer is a great tool to use in investing, it does have its limitations.

Well, it's nice to know that the human brain isn't totally obsolete. What are some of the specific tests you use in picking stocks?

The most important is the 12-month earnings outlook, adjusted for goodwill amortization. We balance that against the long-term and more-recent growth rates for the company and industry, as a reality check. We don't like companies that have disappointed analysts with negative earnings surprises. We want a good fix on how well the company is performing near-term.

As that answer suggests, Gary, though you're known as a "value" manager—and that's the name on your funds—you don't seem to have any theo-

logical hostility to "growth," either. How do you differentiate between those two approaches, and to what extent do you try to blend them?

It's really very simple. As Warren Buffett has said, over the long haul growth and value are the same thing. If, as a "value" investor, you focus too much on just investing in the cheapest stocks you can find, you end up with a garbage portfolio that doesn't perform very well. So we rank our universe of stocks on how strong their business fundamentals are, and throw out the bottom third—no matter how low their valuations seem. Conversely, at the other end of the spectrum, we throw out the 20% or 25% that are most richly valued, that trade for more than 25 or 30 times the next 12 months' earnings—no matter how rapidly they're growing. That still leaves an enormous amount of companies in the middle.

With Robert Sanborn

Robert Sanborn has grown a few chin whiskers since I last interviewed him a couple of years ago, but that's the only discernible change in one of Wall Street's *steadiest performers. Even his twins, born in 1994, are balanced (a boy and a girl), and his patient search for bargains has resulted in peer-beating performance for his Oakmark Fund (800-625-6275; no load). It has been a superb choice over the years for those who like to sleep nights and make money, a category that takes in almost all of us.*

Good as he has been for his shareholders, the modest, Boston-born Chicago investor has been even better for readers of my newsletters. From the time I interviewed him in Louis Rukeyser's Mutual Funds *in December 1994 until I introduced him to readers of* Louis Rukeyser's Wall Street *in March 1996, Robert's specific stock recommendations had a stunning average gain of 67.1%; all but one soundly whipped the S&P. And his impressive record has continued since then. Let's face it: this man can pick stocks.*

June 1998

Robert, you're a value investor in what has been a go-go market, but your long-term performance continues to be impressive as measured by both risk and reward. Is this market more diverse than it's usually characterized?

Actually, Lou, we feel pretty lucky that we've been able

to achieve this record in this market. To be honest with
you, I think our fund is better suited for a bad market,
because of the way we invest.

**Skeptics about your fund's future performance say that you now have too
many assets and that this means you are having to invest in larger corporations. Are these accurate comments?**

It's accurate that the fund is large. But it would be
invested virtually identically if it were much smaller. I
think the world is more conducive to large companies than
it was even five or 10 years ago. Large companies have a
very large competitive advantage in the world economy, so
I would have a bias toward the large companies anyhow.
It's also worth noting that the fund's turnover is very low—
20% per year—so it's much easier for us to manage a large
amount of capital than it would be for a heavy-trading
fund.

**So you're not a believer in the theory that small companies are about to take
over market leadership?**

No; I think the long-term trend will continue. The small
companies generally are in a tougher fundamental situation relative to the big companies, and I think this will
dictate their comparative performance over the next 10
years.

**The way you describe your techniques, they're breathtakingly simple: buy
companies for less than their "private market value"—that is, what a knowl-
edgeable investor would pay for the whole business—and then sell them**

when they reach 90% of that value. If it's that easy, why don't more funds match your returns?

I think the tendency is to "do the momentum thing" [chase market favorites] and to be active, whipping the billions around. A lot of people who say they are value investors don't act that way; they are really closet momentum people. We really are hard-core value investors, and we resist the temptation to do the seat-of-the-pants kind of investing. ■

Try 3 Issues of My Newsletters—FREE!

How Many Economists Does It Take to Screw in a Lightbulb?

BY LOUIS RUKEYSER

For nearly three decades, I've been in the business of helping other people get rich. Now I'd like to do the same for you, with *Louis Rukeyser's Wall Street* and *Louis Rukeyser's Mutual Funds.*

Every month, these unique investment services give you my exclusive insights on what really lies ahead for investors—and how you personally can profit.

Whether it's my winning forecasts on interest rates... how most profitably to ride the high-tech roller coaster... the shifting prospects for healthcare, financial and retail stocks... the best ways to generate a high and steady income stream... or whether inflation—and gold—are finally ready for a comeback, I'll be giving you my personal guidance—straight and to the point.

And the Rest of the Best in Wall Street, Too!

In every issue of *Louis Rukeyser's Wall Street*, I provide a broad, usable overview of where we all stand as investors. I guide you to the key strategies of when and how to invest, and bring in the most accomplished people in the business to give you specific recommendations.

As you'll see, I call only on Wall Street's proven producers. And I make sure these investing All-Stars tell us in plain English—not Wall-Street-speak—exactly how they're adjusting their own portfolios.

What You'll Get Every Month in *Louis Rukeyser's Wall Street*

• You'll get my *personal unhedged views* on the vital investment currents of the day and the surest ways to turn them into money for yourself.
• Top industry analysts and fund managers will give you their single *favorite growth stock* for the year ahead.
• You'll get the frank views of *the best investment thinkers on earth*—the very few genuine titans of finance—men and women who warmly share my view on the importance of getting in and staying in with the right stocks.
• You'll get *specific bond picks* from the most sought-after fixed-income experts in Wall Street.
• You'll see *where to park your cash* for safe, high (and often tax-free) income, now that CD and money-market rates are so low.
• You'll get the *inside report* on what corporate insiders are doing with their own money.

And There's Another Great Newsletter for Mutual-Fund Investors!

It hasn't been easy being a mutual-fund investor lately. In recent years, nine out of 10 stocks funds have failed even to match the unmanaged S&P 500. But a few superlative managers tend to win year after year. To uncover these rare standouts, I launched an unprecedented investment letter: *Louis Rukeyser's Mutual Funds*—the perfect companion to *Louis Rukeyser's Wall Street.*

My fund letter focuses on the flesh-and-blood people who make the decisions with your money. Remember, people make mutual funds, not vice versa. In sailing regattas every racer has an identical boat, but a few skilled sailors still win most of the races. *Louis Rukeyser's Mutual Funds* brings you the select few skippers worthy of sailing *your* financial vessel.

What You'll Get Every Month in *Louis Rukeyser's Mutual Funds*

1) Your Money Will Be in the Hands of the Best and the Brightest in the Business. I'll introduce you to the few managers who have consistently enriched their clients. You'll really get to know the managers minding your cash... what kind of people they are... which investments they like... which they don't... how risk-oriented they are... how conservative. This will give you a comfort level most investors will never enjoy.

2) You'll See What's in Your Funds. We'll let you in on the specifics of each manager's favorite holdings. You

don't want to own a fund with a huge amount of stock you'd never buy yourself!

3) You'll Learn How to Lighten Your Loads. Plus take advantage of a lot of other little tricks my friends inside the mutual-fund industry share with me. For instance, if you know the magic words, you can even get into a fund that's closed to new investors.

4) You'll Diversify Right. It's not enough to buy a bunch of funds and consider yourself diversified. There's a right way and a wrong way to generate the higher gains true diversification brings.

5) I'll Tip You Off to Misleading Ads and Rip-Off Artists. I'll alert you to bogus ads and misleading marketing. I'll also warn you of hidden fees like high 12b-1 fees, exit charges and other disguised loads. Many newspa-

per and magazine articles over the years have called me "the champion of the small investor." If the advice I give you each month in my fund letter helps even the playing field between the big-bucks crowd and you, I'll feel I've earned my title all over again.

Let Me Send You Three Free Issues So You Can Judge for Yourself

See for yourself why hundreds of thousands of happy subscribers consider *Louis Rukeyser's Wall Street* and *Louis Rukeyser's Mutual Funds* the best investment advice available anywhere— and have made them by far the most popular financial newsletters in the world. Just call 800-892-9702 (or mail the coupon) and I'll send you the next three issues of either newsletter absolutely free— with no obligation, plus an invitation to subscribe at half the regular rate—or even less!

Get the Best Advice in Wall Street Now! Call 800-892-9702

OK Lou, I'll take you up on your offer to send me three free issues. If I decide that your letter is not for me—and I am the sole judge of that—I will write "cancel" on the invoice and send it back. That will end the matter—with no cost or obligation. With that understanding, here's what I'd like:

☐ Please send me three free issues of *Louis Rukeyser's Wall Street* and then start my one-year **half-price** subscription for $49.50 (regular rate: $99).

☐ Please send me three free issues of *Louis Rukeyser's Mutual Funds* and then start my one-year **less-than-half-price** subscription for $39 (regular rate: $96).

☐ **BEST DEAL!** **Give me both for less!** I want the complete winning package. Send me three free issues of *both* your letters and bill me just $78.50—a $10 savings off the individual discount prices.

Name_____

Address_____

City_____ State _____ ZIP_____

call **800-892-9702**
or mail to
FSA, 1750 Old Meadow Rd, #300, McLean, VA 22102